The American Invasion

THE
AMERICAN
INVASION

Francis Williams

CROWN PUBLISHERS, INC.

NEW YORK

TO JESS
Who shared it all

© Copyright 1962 by Francis Williams

Author's Foreword: to the American Edition
This Invasion Is World-wide

THE AMERICAN INVASION is going on all over the world: American ideas, American methods, American customs, American habits of eating, drinking and dressing, American amusements, American social patterns, American capital. They move across all frontiers—even those of the Communist countries.

Wherever you go in Europe, in Asia, in Africa, in Australasia, in the Middle East, you are conscious of the invasion. In some areas it moves forward with the massive and seemingly irresistible force of an impersonal take-over bid. In others it is as yet no more than a preliminary infiltration—a promise of what is to come.

This book deals in detail with the American invasion of Britain because that is where I live and where I know best what is happening. But although in terms of investment, of businesses taken over, industries controlled, advertising dominated, this invasion has now gone farther in Britain than in most other countries except Canada, you could duplicate British experience in some degree in most countries in Europe and in larger or smaller measure and varying form in most other major and minor countries in the world outside the Communist bloc. Even there the American invasion, although less tangible, is in some ways—and particularly among the young—hardly less pervasive, as you find out when you meet a Russian teen-age group.

American civilisation has become in its material aspects a matrix and model for the world. But what the world is offered is an export model, not the indigenous form. And an export model that tends to concentrate on particular aspects of this civilisation and in some ways to caricature it.

Because of its consequences in so many directions and its potential, and indeed already actual, effect on much of the pattern of British society, I have dealt in detail in the opening chapters of this book with the immense increase in American control of important sections of British industry over the past ten years—an aspect of the American invasion whose extent is certainly not fully realised by the average citizen of Britain nor, I should guess, by the average citizen of the United States.

But although American investment in British business has nearly trebled in the last ten years, Britain is far from being alone in finding more and more of its economy coming under American control, particularly those sectors directly related to consumer demand and therefore likely to influence the buying and living habits of ordinary people markedly.

Britain has taken the first brunt of the American post-war capital invasion. But in Europe as a whole American business investment is more than double what it was ten years ago, and direct investment in European manufacturing plants—usually carrying with it control—has gone up a good deal more. The same is true elsewhere. American investment in industries throughout the world was around $11,700,000,000 in 1950—nearly double what it was before the war. By 1959 it had risen to over $29,700,000,000. It is probably now close on $35,000,000,000 and is still rising.

Wherever you go from Germany to Japan, from the Middle East to the new African countries, Latin America to Australia, the Mediterranean to the Pacific, you will find American capital backed by American know-how and American advertising moving in.

This capital invasion, important though it is for its direct—and indirect —consequences, is of course only one part of the American invasion. The impact of American ideas, and still more, American social attitudes and ways of life, is even more profound and all-pervasive than that of American investment capital. Sometimes it hits you as soon as you arrive in a country—you see it in the stores and office blocks, in the theatres and apartment houses, in the way people talk and dress and behave and the things they read. Sometimes you need to have known a country years before to be aware of the changes Americanisation has wrought. But if you travel about the world a good deal you cannot but be aware of it in some shape or form almost wherever you go.

It is carried by American books, American magazines, American films, American television: the new television stations now coming into existence in the emergent nations of Africa carry for most of their viewing time the American programmes you saw in the States years ago—and a very curious view of American life many of them give.

The American image backed by the immense resources of mass communication and industrial techniques has become the most potent influence in the history of the world, transcending differences of race and culture and history and even of political ideology.

This is so, of course, not only because of the power and wealth and vigour of American life itself but because the whole world is moving inevitably towards greater industrialisation and more standardised consumption. The rate of movement is not equal in all aspects of life. The old jostles the new so that in the shadow of the oil wells or the great new irrigation projects built by American engineers on the Arabian desert you may find the black tents of the Bedouins and see men tilling the unfruitful earth with a wooden plough drawn by an ox, as you could have done centuries ago, or find, as I have done, in a Lap tent in the Arctic

Circle a small boy playing with a toy sub-machine gun "guaranteed" to have come from Chicago.

But although the pace varies, the march towards industrialisation inexorably proceeds—towards industrialisation and "Americanisation." It is natural that the two should seem to go hand in hand because to most of the world, America—for good or ill—represents the epitome of modern industrialisation, of a society geared above all else to mass consumption. What tends to be thought of all over the world as an American invasion is therefore sometimes, in part at least, the consequence not of direct or even indirect American influence but the natural outcome of an historical trend of which the United States happens to be the most admired—or hated—exemplar. America gets the credit, or the blame, for a process which is world-wide and derives inevitably from the climate of the age, so that industrialisation in Soviet Russia—despite the deep ideological and political differences between the two countries—is bound to resemble in its technological and even in many of its social aspects American industrialisation more nearly than anything else, and to borrow willingly or unwillingly, consciously or unconsciously, more from America than any other country.

But although this is true, although the industrial revolution of the second half of the twentieth century with all its consequences on the social mores of our times would proceed even if there were no American capital invasion on the scale that is now taking place, and no incessant, mass-communicated, mass-advertised, consumer-directed bombardment of American attitudes and domestic values, it is only part of the truth.

The American invasion is—or so it seems to an ever-increasing number of people at the receiving end—a conscious invasion also: conscious, that is, so far as many major groups and interests in America are concerned, even if not so for the mass of American people.

Of this there are two things to say—or perhaps three.

One is that in so far as it is a planned and conscious invasion inspired, in part at any rate, by the desire to find more profitable outlets for American capital and American know-how, it often seems to aim at remodelling other societies to an American pattern at a speed and to a degree that is dangerous for them and could be dangerous for the world, including America. The drive to create a consumer market as nearly identical to the American as possible—and that such a drive is the motive behind a good deal of the invasion seems clear from the special pattern of American investment in Britain as described in later chapters—ignores far too often the ecology of social systems: the inter-relation of history and geography and tradition and the slow mellowing of national character. Civilisations can learn from each other and borrow from each other. They have done so continuously thoughout the ages. But they cannot be transplanted in their entirety from one setting to another. An All-American world, if such a thing were possible, would not be a better world. Quite irrespective of the merits or demerits of American civilisation, it would be a worse one.

The second thing to remark is that although no one in his senses in Western Europe, and indeed in Africa and Asia too, is not conscious of the immense American contribution to human well-being since the war and grateful for the generosity of the American spirit in its approach to vast international problems, they have a great deal of fear of being swamped by America. This may be unjustified. It may in some instances represent no more than a strangled protest at the way the world, willy nilly, is going. But it is there. It exists. And it would be sensible for Americans to recognize it more than they sometimes seem to do.

One cannot travel about the world without constantly being made aware of the immense ambivalence of popular mood towards America. Although this love-hate relationship often upsets travelling Americans conscious only of their own desire to be friendly it should not surprise anyone. It has nothing basically to do with politics or with American policy: although sometimes the form in which that policy is expressed adds to it. It exists at a deeper human level than alliances—or conflicts—between Governments and it is nothing so simple as anti-Americanism, although that is sometimes the form it seems to take.

I think this feeling exists less in Britain than in most other countries, for a whole host of reasons connected with the long links between the two countries and a good deal of common background. But it would be foolish to deny that it is not to be found here as elsewhere nor that it is not increased by much of the current scope and nature of the American invasion. Officially it is not regarded as a very respectable emotion and therefore many people on both sides of the Atlantic try to pretend that it does not exist. But to be honest—and it is sensible to be honest in such matters—it does. And indeed it would be surprising if it did not.

This ambivalence which is to be found, often in much greater measure than in Britain, in every country where the pressure of the American mode is growing—and that means the larger part of the world—is born on the one hand of the immense pull of American material success, the sense of an abounding civilisation in which the standard of living of most ordinary people has climbed to heights undreamed of in most earlier societies, and on the other, of the feeling that the price to be paid for this success may be so high in terms of its effect on the rich variety of human life that it cannot be paid without loss of national personality. It may seem insulting to say that the world is full of people who wish they could have some of the things America has without having to be American, and are terrified that they can't—but it is true. It is a natural enough feeling. People have an affection for their own identity. The feeling is swollen by the sense that behind the American invasion there often lies, either for ideological reasons or as a matter of plain commercial interest in selling, an American conviction that people in other countries ought to be made more like Americans. That they need to be taught to buy and feel and behave and think in the American way—and that not to want to do this is wrong-headed or even immoral.

The feeling that this is what America wants may well be quite contrary to the real attitude of many ordinary Americans—I have no doubt it is—but it is the impression conveyed by a great many American business and advertising techniques abroad. If it is a wrong impression I think the American people ought to take note of it and do something to correct it. To report it as a matter of objective fact is part of the purpose of this book by one who believes that what I have called the export model of American civilisation often falls a long way short of true American civilisation.

This brings me to the third thing I think worth saying. Although stated in a British context in this book because that happens to be the context I know best, it has equal relevance for other countries: indeed, although some of the examples would be different and some of the emphasis changed, much of this book could just as well have been written by a Frenchman, or a German, a Canadian, an Australian, an Indian or a West African as by an Englishman. Since it was first published in an English edition many have written to say so.

But to this third point.

The pressure of American influence on the rest of the world is inevitably concentrating more and more fascinated world attention on aspects of American life which—rightly or wrongly—it is suspected may come along with the package deal. Some of them are dealt with in this book. You may feel that they give a very partial picture of American life. And, as I have tried to say in many places in the body of the book itself, you will be right.

I have had the good fortune to spend many of the happiest hours of my life in America and the luck to live for several prolonged periods in your country. Many of the American friendships I am proud to have are among the most entrancing and enriching I have known.

I am well aware, because I have had experience of it, of the depth and variety of a great deal of American life, of its warmth and friendliness, its vivacity and intellectual energy, its open-handed generosity to the stranger, its abounding good-will. I have written, I hope, as one whose affection for America and admiration for its immense contribution to the world's well-being go too deep for it to be necessary to be less than honest in reporting on the way some facets of American life strike those—many without any direct personal knowledge of America—who watch with strongly divided feelings the impress of American society upon their own and ask themselves how far certain trends in this society—comparatively recent but as it seems from a distance, growing in strength—may be the inevitable consequence of American invasion.

The aspects of American life I have dwelt on are therefore selective and partial, for they are confined almost entirely to those that most worry non-Americans as they contemplate the force of the American impact on the world. Perhaps it is right to be worried by them. Perhaps not. But for good or ill, whether you mind or not, they contribute enormously to the face America now presents to the world.

I am well aware that a similar picure of Britain could be drawn from a similar standpoint with even less favourable results. I have no doubt I should find it often disagreeable to read and be irritated, as you may well be, by what would strike me as distortions of vision and failures in perspective. But this is not an attempt at a portrait in the round. That would have produced a much more cheerful picture and been a lot more agreeable to do. It is with certain features of American life deriving, or so it seems to an outsider, from economic and social assumptions made by American big business, American advertising, American mass entertainment that it is concerned, because they are being transmitted with steadily increasing force overseas.

Revisiting America for six months last year, it was the change in American society over the last ten years that most struck me: and to be frank, the extent to which it seemed to an outsider to becoming more standardised, more stratified, less enterprising, less intellectually and socially· adventurous. You may think I am wrong about this. I hope I am. In any event America is so big and has such immense reserves of creative energy to turn to, that the changes that hit me with such force may be no more than passing phenomena.

But for those on the other side of the hill any change in the human climate of America, a hardening of the social arteries, as it seemed to me, cannot but have a relevance to their own condition. If this is what the American invasion would mean to them, they are right to be doubtful about it. If it would not, then I hope America will do something to set the record straight before too late.

What you are offered here is an intelligence report on an invasion seen from the other side. If events prove it wrong no one will be happier than I. But the invasion itself is a fact and it is world-wide. It is time you considered its consequences on your relationship with the rest of the world.

Contents

1

Benevolent Eagle

THE American Eagle is a friendly bird. It does not wish to swoop upon the little lambs. It desires only to help them to be good. Beneficient although not harmless, its wings cast their shadows over Grosvenor Square and in ever-widening circles across the Western sky.

To complain of the world-wide advance of American power is silly. Such an advance is inevitable in the current nature of the world. Successive British Governments have done everything they could to invoke it for reasons that seemed and still seem politically sound. It is not for us to complain because our efforts to bring America permanently into Europe have succeeded.

But need alliance involve occupation? Must we become Americans to save Western civilization? These are not merely rhetorical questions. The impact of American ideas, and still more of American ways of life, is now so large, the drive of America to Americanize so great, that to ask how much of what is specifically English in our civilization will remain in a decade or two if the trend continues is by no means absurd. Moreover, as the facts set out in subsequent chapters will show, the American invasion is now taking on a much more explicit form than previously. The dollars are moving in behind the ideas. In that expressive phrase used by Americans when they decide, as they so often do, to remodel their kitchens, Britain, and much of Europe besides, is being made over.

There are many, both American and British, who think it right that this should be so. To them not to want, in the second half of the twentieth century, to live like Americans is a sign of a deviation from the desirable norm so great as to bring suspicion not only on one's intelligence but one's morals. Yet even in America there are some who think otherwise. As they drive their regulated way in the designated traffic lane, mile after ordered mile along the vast freeways that lacerate their country, or, as happens increasingly to the more timid in Los Angeles and some other great cities, cower at home immobilized by the immense mobility of the society in which they live, these permit themselves to hope that somewhere a land will remain (preferably English-speaking) in which it will still be possible to recall other and older values than rapid mobility and conspicuous expenditure.

This is not because they are antagonistic to their own society. On the contrary, loving what is best in it, and the best is very good, but recognizing also the historical, ethnological and geographical drives within it towards an assembly belt civilization processed to prevent Americans from 'being stoopid', they also appreciate the specific characteristics of other cultures and know that an All-American world would be the last sad surrender to conformity.

Because this book is concerned with the extent of the American invasion, I hope no one will make the mistake of thinking it anti-American. Sir Harold Nicholson once remarked that Americans are sometimes easy to dislike but always difficult not to love. My love affair with them is of long duration. I cannot claim to know the whole of their immense and exhilarating country but in the past fifteen or sixteen years I have been in twenty States and travelled many thousands of miles and some of the best times of my life have been spent there.

But the best of American life, like the best of English or French life, is not for export. At least it does not often get exported. What too often moves across the world in the wake of American money and American know-how is what is most brash and superficial; a surface way of life which although truly and overpoweringly American derives not from the deeper virtues of American character but from those influences which have most markedly shaped it in the public domain; the hurrying, unfinished impetus of its amalgamation of races, its war against the hostility of space and distance, the need to assure itself that it has the key to a happiness elsewhere unattainable.

Much of the actual writing of this book, as it happens, has been done inside the territory of the invading forces themselves – on a patio in California close to the enchantments of San Francisco and the Golden Gate. I had just started on it when the University of California at Berkeley – one of the great universities of America which counts its Nobel prizewinners as lesser institutions do their football stars – did me the honour of inviting me to visit its Campus as Regents' Professor. I hope that the friends I made in Berkeley will not regard anything here as an ungenerous response to their kindness. If in its pages they find, as they well may do, cautionary examples drawn from the Californian scene of the horrors to which American civilization can sometimes come they will recognize, I know, that this is only because their great and lovely State carries so much of the future in its arms that it is bound to present to the astonished eye of the beholder some of the worst as well as much of the best of American life.

What I am concerned with in this book is not America as it affects Americans, except in so far as that is relevant to the results on a society of some of the things we are invited to emulate – but America as it affects, or can affect, the people of other countries and particularly, of course, the British. This is an intelligence report on an invasion. No doubt the invasion is benevolent. But that does not make it less threatening. There are few things so menacing as wholesale benevolence. To know one's friends is as necessary as to know one's enemies; especially when they bear gifts.

To many kindly and well-meaning Americans the term invasion will seem ungrateful and insulting. They see what is taking place not as an invasion but as a liberation and expect a due response. (We who are about to be liberated salute you.) But whether invasion or liberation, what is now happening could of its nature require great changes in many British habits and ways of life.

I should perhaps explain at the beginning that the million or so American service men scattered glumly about the world with their wives and families have little place in this report. This may seem a strange omission to those absorbed in the dialectics and anxieties of the cold war to whom the physical presence of American troops on foreign soil seems, for good or ill, the primary American fact of our times. To me it is no more than an unavoidable part of the logistics of our age. I cannot share the opinion of those who consider American bases in Britain and on the Continent an incitement to war. On the contrary they seem to me, in the world as it is, a possible safeguard of peace. In any event this book is not about international politics, or American and Russian military power, or the tactics of the cold war, but about the impact of American civilization on the world. And in that, American service men and their wives have, in Britain at any rate, little part.

Segregated behind fences in the demi-paradise of their own compounds, able to buy in the P.X. everything they have learned to look for in the friendly neighbourhood super-market (all-American consumer organizations from super-markets to morticians are friendly by definition), safeguarded from the contamination of foreign food by air transport and deep freezes, they live their well-paid lives neither compelled nor encouraged to make unnecessary contact with the natives. An occasional rape, a brawl now and then at a dance hall, a trickle of traffic offences; apart from these – the congenital misfortunes of all overseas armies – they make little impact on their surroundings. They lack, for the most part it would seem, either the talent or the inclination to put down roots in foreign climes. Those who do emerge into the open are usually to be seen, lost and lonely, at the street corners of provincial cities; bored, pathetic, and seemingly, for the most part, incurably adolescent; sick with a peculiarly American homesickness – the least assimilating and assimilated army in history. One cannot help but feel sorry for them, so untutored in showing their virtues to a world so many of whose burdens they have been called upon to shoulder.

Nor need we spend much time, I think, on the great civilian

army of U.S. officials who, bringing their hygienic toilet paper and prejudices with them, have settled like charitable locusts in so many lands to fight the good fight against Communism by attending each other's cocktail parties. Amiable, innocent, well-meaning and incurably aware of the superiority of the American way of life, some of them have done a good deal of damage to the image of American civilization in many parts of the world. I have watched them doing it in the Middle East and elsewhere with the wry discomfort one used to reserve for the more pompous antics of the British. No doubt here and there they have also done some good. But although those in Britain are friendly and able and have an advantage that many of their colleagues in other countries seem to lack in being able to speak the language of the country to which they are accredited, London is too big for them to have much part in affecting the picture of their country held by the English.

They move across the surface of society, welcoming and welcome. But the American invasion with which this book is concerned is more powerful and pervasive than anything that finds expression in diplomatic get-togethers or the long-drawn platitudes of Pilgrims' dinners and banquets organized by the English-Speaking Union. Let us consider just what it already amounts to.

2

Dollars on the Move

IN the last ten years the investment of American big business in British industry has nearly trebled. It is now more than ten times what it was before the war and is increasing at an average rate of well over thirteen and a half per cent annually – getting on for £170,000,000 a year. By the end of 1960 the total American investment here had climbed to around £1,110,000,000 according to estimates by the United States Department of Commerce. It is now probably close on £1,250,000,000. More American money is invested in British industry than in that of any other country in the world except Canada, where the extent of American influence on the national economy has become a matter of major political concern. And practically all this mounting investment carries with it management control of British business.

This American take-over bid is a post-war phenomenon: in the mid thirties total American investment in British industry was around £169,000,000, only £97,000,000 in manufacturing – less than is pouring in afresh each year now. It is gaining momentum all the time. It began slowly in the immediate post-war years, increasing by an average of about 5·6 per cent each year up to 1949. In the next five years the rate of increase doubled. Since then it has jumped again. It rose by an average of 13·6 per cent each year between 1954 and 1959. According to estimates by Dr.John H. Dunning,author of "American Investment In British Manufacturing Industry" and the leading authority in this field, it must be expected to continue at least at the same rate of expansion over the next ten years.

This flow of American money is going particularly into consumer industries and specialised manufacturing operations of key importance to the future shape of our economy. American big business is giving British economy a new look and a highly profitable one for those concerned – the average return on American industrial assets in Britain is estimated to be over $16\frac{1}{2}$ per cent compared with only just over $10\frac{1}{2}$ per cent in the United States itself.

According to U.S. Department of Commerce figures close on 800 British industrial and business firms – many of them the biggest in their fields, giants in any language – are already under American control. The total value of the net assets of those engaged on manufacturing alone, without taking into account other large scale business activities, was estimated by Dr. Dunning to be at least £120,000,000,000 at the end of 1960. Already one-twentieth of all the goods produced by British workers comes from American-owned plants. So do more than one-tenth of all our exports of manufactured goods. One out of every twenty British workers in the manufacturing industries now has an American employer. And the number is increasing all the time. Since the war the total labour force in British manufacturing as a whole has increased by 40 per cent. But the labour force in American financed firms has risen by 175 per cent. And behind these American firms in Britain there are parent companies spending on research and market development more than the whole of British industry put together. They have made it plain that they intend to increase their share of British markets even more. 'One of the significant marks of the year' said Mr. Reginald Maudling, then President of the Board of Trade, in a pamphlet issued by that Ministry at the end of 1960 'has been the evident wish of important United States manufacturers to increase their stake in British economy.' We are in the middle of the biggest economic invasion in our history.

This is not an invasion by little people. More than fifty per cent of American investment in British industry is in the hands of ten of the giants of American big business, among them General Motors, Vacuum Oil, Standard Oil of New Jersey, Proctor and Gamble, Ford Motors, Monsanto Chemicals and Goodyear Tyre and Rubber. Those who direct the advance are the men and groups who control economic power in the United States and know exactly what they are doing.

What they are doing at present is to get a grip on the more profitable sections of British business. In November 1960 the Ford bid turning the British Ford Motor Company into a wholly-owned subsidiary of American Ford hit the headlines with considerable clamour. But it was only the latest of a number of American take-overs. Among the biggest of these were the deals by which, despite the opposition of the most influential group of British merchant bankers ever brought together in and around Threadneedle Street to repel an invader (the King Penguins of the City in full panoply), Reynolds Metal of America secured control of Britain's biggest aluminium company, British Aluminium, and that by which the American controlled tractor firm, Massey-Ferguson of Canada, moved in on the finest tractor plant in all Europe, that jointly owned by Perkins and Standard Motors. But these are only the big ones that hit the headlines. There have been scores of others.

Little or no American investment is going into the older British industries. Cotton and shipbuilding, for example, are left alone. They have passed their zenith. The financial invaders are content to leave them in the hands of the native owners. American capital is interested only in expanding industries. They are backing their judgement that as living standards rise further the pattern of British economy and British society will become closer and closer to that of the American and that there will be a rapid increase in the market for American-type products.

This American invasion of the British economy has already gone much farther than most people in Britain realize. Despite the publicity given to one or two of the biggest deals like Ford's and British Aluminium it has been in the main a silent invasion. It has been directed primarily to consumer industries and those where the technological revolution of the 'sixties can have most play.

Here are some of the main industries in which there is already a heavy concentration of American finance, backed in most cases by management by American nationals transferred from the States to occupy key positions, particularly in top administration and sales promotion, and to train personnel in American methods:

Pharmaceutical drugs, office appliances, food products, automobiles and automobile accessories, electronics, toilet preparations, printing machinery, plastics, electrical switchgear, foundation garments, safety razors, proprietory medicines, precision instruments, refrigerators, washing machines, kitchen equipment, cosmetics, detergents and soap products, nickel alloys, petroleum products, motor tyres, dictating and recording machines, heating appliances, electrical instruments and control gear, photographic films, sewing machines, scientific instruments, hair shampoos, laundry and dry-cleaning machinery, fountain pens and desk sets, insulating materials, air-conditioners, lifts and escalators, cutlery and hardware, cigarette lighters, earth-moving machinery, agricultural machinery, soft drinks, dental goods, mechanical handling equipment, chemicals, canned animal food, pneumatic tools.

The list could be extended. The range is wide. But there is one common denominator. They are all growth industries. And most of them are new.

Despite the rapid rate of increase in the last ten years the American invasion of the British economy is even yet only in its initial stages. Wall Street brokerage firms and investment consultants are sending a steady stream of men to London to plot out the land and report on fresh opportunities for American take-over. Three-quarters of the banker members of the New York Clearing House Association now have branches in the City on the look-out for business.

If the current rate of investment continues the American stake in British industry will be more than double what it now is in another eight years.

Already American financed firms have secured a dominating position in many of the consumer trades.

Half the cosmetics British women now put on their faces are sold to them by American-owned firms. The English complexion, justly famed for so long in so many lands, is coming out of an American bottle.

Nor is the English figure any more free of American influence. Two-thirds of all the foundation garments – the corsets, the suspender belts, the brassieres – bought in Britain are supplied by eight American-controlled firms.

So is a considerable part of the diet that keeps the figure trim.

Four American-owned firms to all intents and purposes monopolize the breakfast cereals market. With every snap, crackle and pop on the breakfast table the American accent carries farther.

Three-quarters of the processed cheese products consumed here are produced by two American companies, almost all the custard eaten by another three. Canned goods, cake mixes, soft drinks – the American influence is dominant in all of them.

More than half the drugs supplied through the National Health Service are supplied by thirteen American-owned firms who, according to one authoritative trade paper for pharmaceutical chemists, send close on fifty per cent of what these drugs cost the N.H.S. back to America (which has of course no Health Service of its own) in dollar profits. The output of antibiotic drugs other than penicillin is almost an American monopoly. In his research survey, already referred to, Dr. Dunning noted that up to 1957 most of the major post-war developments in this field had emanated from American firms.

A large proportion of the patent medicines, ointments, antiseptics and tonics of one kind and another bought by British men and women likewise come from American-owned firms, more than a score of which are active in this market.

The largest share of the vast new market for detergents, constantly inflated by immense advertising expenditure, is held by two American companies, Thomas Hedley, which is a wholly owned subsidiary of Proctor and Gamble, and Colgate Palmolive.

Between them they spend well over £6,500,000 a year on advertising, over £5,880,000 of it on commercial television. And it is perhaps significant that their biggest competitor in this field, Unilever, decided in September 1961 to bring over an American marketing expert with particular experience of commercial television to a top job on its Marketing–Management Committee.

Most of the electric washing machines in which the detergents are put are also American. So are a large proportion of the vacuum cleaners, refrigerators, sewing machines, steam irons, pressure cookers and electric mixers in British kitchens.

The machines to wash the clothes and the detergents to put in the machines to wash the clothes; the gleaming white refrigerators and the cans and packaged foods to put in the gleaming white refrigerators; the gadgets and culinary implements to make the turning of the packaged foods into tasty meals, all these and many more aids to modern living of a like kind are high in the baggage train of the United States army of liberation which moves so purposefully into British markets.

Nor are men ignored. Nine out of every ten who shave themselves with safety razors in the morning do so by courtesy of American blades. If they use an electric razor they are likely to be almost equally in America's debt. And it is an even bet that when they come home in the evening they will use American tools produced by American subsidiaries in Britain for the do-it-yourself jobs their wives have waiting for them – and light a cigarette with an American lighter before they start.

In the bathroom, in the kitchen, in the bedroom and the dining-room, in the lounge and the garage, American products – some carrying good British names – influence our habits for good or ill.

Two out of every five cars on British roads come from American-owned plants. Of the four largest manufacturers of tyres in Britain three are U.S. controlled.

The key to the world of spiralling consumer demand created by American industry is advertising. Advertising has gone far beyond mere salesmanship to become one of the chief creators and communicators of social values in our time. Its artists and copy writers are the priests and ballad singers of our day.

And among the biggest advertising agents in Britain – far

ahead of most competitors in the volume of business it handles
– is the American J. Walter Thompson Co. It places more than
£14,750,000 of advertising a year and significantly is almost the
only big agency to spend more on Commercial Television than
in the press. Another American-controlled advertising agency,
Erwin Wasey, Ruthrauff and Ryan, has advertising billings getting
on for £8,250,000 a year. A third, McCann-Erickson, already
well established here, has recently added to its size by taking over
one of the best known and best thought of British agencies,
Pritchard Word with billings of over £3,600,000. These are only,
a few of the big agencies backed by American money and
American techniques.

Almost every week the advertising trade press carries news of
fresh American entries into the British advertising industry. 'I
am tired of hearing of British agencies selling out to American
concerns or effecting mergers which lead to them being run from
across the Atlantic,' declared the head of one Britich Agency,
Col. George Warden, announcing in the middle of 1961 the
formation of a private trust to keep control of his own company
in British hands. Nor can even the strongest of the British
agencies and the firms they act for stand aside from the impact of
American methods on advertising practice.

What British families should be taught to feel and think in
order to persuade them to spend, has more and more become
the prerogative of American advertising men or their disciples.
They know what the business is about. And what it is about in
American terms has been made plain by Mr. Earl Puckett, chairman of one of the largest of American retail merchandising
groups. 'Our job,' he told an advertising convention, 'is to make
women unhappy with what they have. We must make them so
unhappy that their husbands can find no happiness or peace in
unnecessary saving.'

As one walks through one of the new towns or suburbs that
express the current domestic hopes of the British one is at once
made aware of how much headway this American ambition has
already made. These suburbs have already learnt to buy the
American way. American packaged goods bought in American-

type supermarkets, American labour-saving devices bought on
hire-purchase, American clothes for teenagers, all these and many
other American goods and fashions are turning, if they have not
already turned, the suburbs of a large part of southern and
midland England – the North is on the whole more tenacious –
into an annexe of Main Street where it is always necessary to
have something new. When an M.P. of my acquaintance, who
lives in one of the new towns near London, went to America
ten years ago he felt, he told me, that he was in a foreign country.
But when he went again this year, it was, he said, simply like
walking across the street.

Our civilization is, above all, being re-shaped by the great
American vision of this century – the vision of planned obsolescence. This calls for the deliberate out-dating, by the constant
introduction of new models, of all domestic equipment, TV sets,
automobiles, wearing apparel and anything else to which the
dream of constant 'improvement' can be applied. New ones
must be bought if wives are to be kept happy and husbands hold
up their heads among their fellows.

Obsolescence has become one of the primary instruments of
American business. We have not yet learned to scrap and spend
with the shining conviction that sustains American economy. But
everything possible is being done to persuade us of the moral
rightness of the philosophy expressed by the principal speaker
at the 1961 Convention of the National Automobile Dealers
Association of America, Mr. Whit Hobbs. 'The nation's customers have an overwhelming desire to up-grade themselves and
their kids,' declared Mr Hobbs. 'We are on a great big beautiful
binge. We're spending more money on being young than on
atomic submarines and missiles and nuclear weapons and foreign
aid. We're going to have fun in 'sixty-one if it kills us.'

The British may still be a little suspicious of some aspects of
Mr. Hobbs's fun. But they are moving fast. They have already
learnt to believe they never had it so good.

Nor is it only in many mass consumer products that the
American influence is becoming predominant.

British agriculture is the most mechanized in the world – but between sixty and seventy per cent of all the agricultural machinery it uses is either American produced or made under licence to American specifications.

British offices are equally dominated by American methods. Nearly two-thirds of the calculating machines and duplicators, a large proportion of the filing cabinets and office furniture, more than half the typewriters and nearly half the pens and pencils used by British business are made in American-controlled factories. So are most of the lifts.

In the new field of electronics backed by an investment in research by their parent companies of over $1,000,000,000 a year American-owned firms in Britain are preparing to establish the same kind of lead. They have already done so in the making of precision industrial instruments. In this, one of the most rapidly growing industries in Britain, American influence and money predominate. Since pre-war the numbers employed in the instruments industry has trebled, the value of its output increased eight-fold. American influence has been so dominant in fact that Dr. Dunning estimated in 1957 that only a fraction of the progress made would have been possible if it had not been for U.S. affiliated firms and Anglo-American licensing agreements.

The same is true of another major new post-war industry in Britain – petroleum refining. The largest petroleum refinery in Britain, that at Fawley on Southampton Water, is owned by an American company, Esso Petroleum, which built it at a cost of £35,500,000 ten years ago and has nearly doubled it in size since. Altogether, Esso and another American company, Vacuum Oil, have invested well over £100,000,000 in Britain in the last eight years and now supply a third of all the petrol used by private motorists and commercial users in Britain.

It was Esso, incidentally, which initiated the system of the tied petrol service station supplying only one brand in return for a special sales rebate which has swept British roads like the plague.

Twelve oil refineries have been built in Britain since the war at a cost of well over £200,000,000. The design, engineering and construction of all these refineries has been in the hands of specialist consultant firms, all but one of which are American controlled.

One could continue this record of American expansion in Britain since the war almost indefinitely. Wherever there is a new and developing industry there American business has established a bridgehead.

We are still, of course, some distance away from the position of our oldest and closest relative in the Commonwealth, Canada. There more than fifty-two per cent of the entire industrial economy is now in American hands. The American grip on Canadian industry in fact has reached the stage where the freedom of the Canadian Government to take independent action in major spheres of economic policy in order to deal with unemployment and other important problems has, in the words of *The Times*, been 'substantially circumscribed'.

The intrusion of American capital here cannot in the nature of things reach the same scale as in Canadian economy. But it carries with it some of the same undertones of danger.

Consider, for example, one recent notorious issue which has roused Canadian public opinion to the dangerous position of subservience in which they find themselves.

The Canadian Government, like the British, recognizes mainland China. It encourages trade between the two countries in the interests both of international relations and Canada's economy. Recently a group of Canadian automobile companies with the strong encouragement of the Canadian Government, which was concerned about the level of unemployment in the industry, negotiated a contract for the sale of a substantial number of tractors to China. At once Detroit stepped in. Within a matter of hours the Canadian people were taught that the motor industry is one part of Canada in which the writ of the Canadian Government does not run.

Declaring the transaction to be contrary to *American* (although not Canadian) policy, American automobile manufacturers ordered all their Canadian affiliates to repudiate the contract without further notice. Apart from other considerations Canadian automobile workers were thus denied a sizeable and badly needed opportunity for employment in work favoured by their own Government at a time of mounting unemployment.

Two out of the four biggest motor manufacturers in Britain are now wholly American owned and controlled. Can we be sure that in similar circumstances they would be any more free from interference than the Canadian automobile manufacturers?

After the remarkable case of the six Viscounts the answer to such a question is no longer a matter of conjecture but fact. It is now quite clear that if occasion arises American control over vital elements of British industry will be used in exactly the same way and for exactly the same political purposes as in Canada.

Consider this Viscount case. In December 1961 it was announced that as part of a purely commercial transaction orders had been placed in Britain for six Viscount airliners for delivery to China. The planes concerned were civilian planes free of strategic embargo. The development of trade with mainland China—with which Britain, unlike America, has diplomatic and commercial relations—is an accepted British interest. The sale of the six Viscounts had therefore the full approval of the British Government. It did not, however, find favour in American eyes and on December 8th Mr. Dean Rusk, the U.S. Secretary of State, made it known publicly that the American Government disapproved of the transaction. This public statement was, according to *The Times*, followed by an "unofficial" protest to the British Government expressing the American Government's sharp disagreement with the approval given to the sale. The British Government very sensibly ignored this protest. It repudiated the suggestion that it should intervene against a perfectly proper commercial transaction fully in line with official British policy. So far so good—or bad. Any Government, of course, is perfectly entitled if it so wishes to express its disagreement with another, although few, perhaps, are so apt as American Governments to assume that they have the right to tell friendly nations what they should or should not do.

What followed has a more sinister connotation—especially when seen in the context of the immense expansion of American

interests in a number of key British industries already described.
The British company which is the main supplier of equipment
for the instrument landing system and V.O.R. navigational
beacon receivers fitted in the Viscount is the Standard Telephones
and Cable Company. This equipment is recommended for
world-wide navigational aids as a major contribution to air safety
by the International Civil Aviation Organisation. But Standard
Telephones and Cables, which has total assets of over £14,500,000
and is one of the biggest producers of telecommunications
equipment in Britain, is wholly owned and controlled by the
International Telephone and Telegraph Company of New York
and governmental pressure having failed, this economic power
was now invoked. In January it became known that the International Telephone and Telegraph Company had been alerted
and "cautioned" by the U.S. State Department regarding the
Viscount transaction, although it had no direct concern with the
supply of the equipment involved none of which even was
manufactured under American licence or American patents:
it had been designed in the British factory. Thereupon the International Telegraph and Telephone Company sent instructions
to its British associate, Standard Telephones and Cables, warning
it that it must not provide equipment for any Viscounts intended
for China. By these means, to put it plainly, a deliberate attempt
was made to use American control of a British company to
subvert British Government policy.

Fortunately in this instance it failed. Similar if not identical
equipment was available from British companies not yet under
American control. But who can say that as the American invasion
proceeds similar pressure will not be employed in other industries
in the future: or that a day will not come when it is effective—as
it already has been in Canada. The sharp divergence of view
between Britain and the United States on the recognition of
mainland China is one of the facts of the international situation
that has to be accepted. What ought not to be accepted, as the
Daily Telegraph pointed out in its agreeably outspoken comments
on the Viscount case, is that 'these differences should serve as a
point of attack on an essentially commercial transaction . . . or

that any pressure should be brought to bear on an American-owned company in this country to prevent the supply of air navigation equipment.' Yet this is exactly what happened.

The way in which American economic power was mobilised in this instance is even more relevant to an inquiry into the American invasion when the fact is taken into account that the field of telecommunications and precision instruments is one in which American infiltration has been particularly marked in recent years. Apart from Standard Telephones and Cables, itself, there are now in this and related fields at least nine British companies under American control. Many others are manufacturing under American licences.

Commenting on the repudiation of the Canadian tractor contract I referred to earlier on orders from American automobile firms, the *Washington Post*—a journal more concerned than the State Department sometimes seem to be that America should recognise the sovereign rights of its friends – commented that this was not the only instance in which Canadian public opinion had been given good cause to feel 'that Big Brother has infringed on Canadian sovereignty'. To judge from the case of the Viscounts, British public opinion would be equally well advised to be on guard against such infringements if the American industrial invasion continues.

The industrial and political implications of the American invasion, which are already serious in Canada and potentially so in Britain, are not the only ones that have to be considered. To an extent exceeding any other in history American business is tied to the mass demand of a consumer market. It is significant that the largest concentration of American interests in British economy is in consumer trades whose success depends on persuading a British public to buy – and to some extent behave and think – like an American one.

Of course the total of British investment in American stocks and shares, although sadly depleted by the financial requirements of two wars, is also large. British investment helped to make the United States an industrial nation and it can be argued that what is happening now is that American investors are returning the compliment once paid to their country by British investors. The two movements are not, however, comparable. British investment in America was mainly in capital industries. It helped American industry to build the railroads and make the machines that gave Americans what they wanted. It did not shape their wants. American investment in Britain on the other hand is predominantly in consumer and service industries. Such industries are directly tied to popular demand, or what can be made a popular demand by skilled promotion.

Moreover, to a much greater extent than was ever the case with British investment in American enterprises, what the Americans are buying is management control. American management, American ideas of what can be done to shape consumer demand, American methods in salesmanship and labour relations, move in along with American capital. What American business is seeking to export to Britain is not just money but American civilization and an American way of life. In an economy tied to a spiralling consumer demand this is the necessary concomitant of success.

When Dr. Dunning sent a questionnaire in 1956 to two hundred of the leading American financed firms in Britain he found that in 30 per cent of them half or more than half the Board was American and in 45 per cent more than a quarter. In the great majority of cases, moreover, all decisions of importance and their method of implementation had to be referred back for approval to the American parent company, including all changes in product range or design, advertising policy and the recruitement of senior staff.

This interference still operates at the top level. The Chairman of one of the largest American controlled firms in Britain with whom I was having dinner told me that his opposite number in the States was on the trans-Atlantic phone every day. 'But I had lunch yesterday with X' (Chairman of an even bigger one), he added. 'It was nice to know his chaps were even worse.'

Dr. Dunning found that on principle both American manufacturing techniques and managerial methods relating to production, purchasing, personnel, sales and advertising were assimilated and rigidly adhered to. A number of the British firms questioned commented that 'any new ideas or suggestions which it might put forward to its U.S. associate were squashed or treated with the greatest suspicion and rarely – if ever – acted upon'. Most of the American Managing Directors sent over when British firms were bought up or new subsidiaries launched were ex-sales executives and more American nationals were employed in the sales departments than in any other.

In one typical case where shortly after the war an important British company surrendered a 50 per cent interest in its equity capital to an American corporation, thirty-five key American executives were flown over within a matter of days to take command of all the important branches of the company's activities. British personnel are sent regularly each year to America for training.

In every case of American ownership expenditure on advertising and sales promotion has been sharply increased. The amount spent on advertising alone is three times as high as the share of total industrial output would call for in British terms and in a great many industries schools in American sales methods have been established not only for their own staffs but for those of their principal retail customers.

Nor is it only in British firms directly controlled from America that American methods are taking over. British management itself is steadily acquiring an American accent – even if it is sometimes a phoney one. The management consultants and efficiency experts, the men in the grey flannel suits, are moving deeper and deeper into British business life. Like their American counterparts businessmen here are learning that the unforgivable heresy is to think you know how to run your own business.

A Register of Management and Industrial Consultants was first established in Britain shortly after the end of the war on a model laid down by the Association of Consulting Management Engineers in the United States. At that time, although the Register was swollen by a number of accountancy firms which have since, for professional reasons, withdrawn, the total number of people engaged in management consultancy was just under 300. It is

now, without the staffs of any firms of accountants, close on
1,300 and there are 28 firms engaged in the business, several
of them with strong American affiliations. According to the
Managing Director of one of the largest firms the new profession
is now handling between 800 and 900 consultancy assignments
and the number is steadily increasing. In September 1961 a
Diploma in Management Studies was initiated. Sponsoring it,
Sir David Eccles, whose taste in grey flannel suitings is of course
impeccable, declared: 'We are still way behind the U.S. We
must catch up.'

Along such trails as these – many of them no doubt admirable
in themselves and capable of leading to richer living pastures – the
American invasion makes its pervasive way. How pervasive one
may discover if one visits one of those English towns which by
some combination of circumstances have become peculiarly open
to the impact of American ideas, in consequence, perhaps, of the
decay of traditional industries and the development of new ones.
Such towns represent a microcosm of a society in transition.
In them old and new may be seen and compared side by side.
Burnley, in Lancashire, is one of them.

Burnley was for generations a cotton town, living and working
by, and for, one of the most traditional of British industrial
processes. The houses clustered round the cotton mills in which
not only the men but most of the women worked: a tough,
idiosyncratic, humorous and independent people, lip-reading
their ironic way through the noisy rattle of the looms in the damp
air of the weaving sheds heavy with cotton fluff, and usually
governed in their industrial affairs by what can best be described
as an armed truce with the mill owners to whom they stood in a
relationship more that of sub-contractors working a set of looms
at their own pace than of employees called on to carry out a
strictly disciplined task at speeds required of them by the management.

The conditions of the industry, rough and sometimes brutal
yet conducive to independence, stamped the character of the
town. It was a community in which everyone knew everyone
else. The mill and the chapel were the centres of a society much

more democratic in its attitudes than most in which men and
women drew upon their own resources for happiness. Despite
the ugliness of the back-to-back houses and the cobbled streets
leading up to the bare hills the social life was energetic and out-
going. Within it the family was a tight, self-dependent unit.

Most of the cotton mills are closed now. Some have been
made bankrupt by depression. In others the looms have been
smashed and sold for scrap under a Government compensation
scheme directed to bringing the cotton industry down to a size
economically viable in current conditions. New industries have
been brought in – bright, shining, modern industries making
domestic equipment, radio parts, motor accessories, things of
that sort. Several are American owned.

In the centre of the town a new skyscraper hotel rises above
the mills – the first to be built outside London since the war.
One walks through the wide doors into a lobby that might be
that of an hotel in Chicago or Detroit. The bell-hop takes one up
in the elevator to a room that with its sleek functionalism, its
private bath, telephone and central heating, is a duplicate of
thousands across the American continent. On the top floor there
is an executive suite for the managing directors who fly in to see
how their branch factories are doing. The dining-room has a
chef from Monte Carlo and stays open until midnight. One looks
out of the window expecting to find neon lights along Main
Street: it comes as a shock to find they are not there yet. One
feels suspended between two worlds.

In the town the cotton mills stand empty and derelict. The vast
floor space of the weaving sheds echoes to the feet with the
hollowness of the abandoned. They are no use to the new
industries which require space for parking lots for the cars of the
workers who come in from miles away in the American fashion.
These new industries build on the periphery. Inside them everything is bright and clean. The damp humidity of the weaving
sheds has been replaced by an air-conditioned purified atmosphere. Working to a schedule exactly contrived by the most
scientific methods of time and motion study to secure the
maximum output suited to their aptitude the women workers

sit in bright, crisp nylon overalls doing the same thing over and over and over.

Transferred to this clinical perfection from their former jobs in the weaving sheds some of the women operators have been so ungrateful as to have nervous breakdowns. But the majority are happy in their work. It leaves them with unengaged minds. They can dream while their fingers follow their intricate but repetitive patterns. I asked one of them what she thought about. 'My boy-friend and going to America,' she said. And another. 'I think of my new hair-do and what's on the telly and why can't we have some of those drug stores they have in America?'

Outside the factory the parked cars give an American air to the scene. When the shift ends most of the cars turn outward away from the town. The old social life, born of the close community of home and mill and chapel, is shrinking. So far there is nothing much to replace it. 'If we are going to be an American town,' said one Councillor, 'then we shall have to have American amenities. Supermarkets, soda-fountains, late-night cinemas – the lot.'

An American town? Well, not quite. 'It's still sort of slow,' said the eager executive from Southern California who runs one of the American-owned plants. 'But you can feel things moving. The people are getting more like those back home. They're buying cars and going places. They shop around for jobs. They're more competitive and restless than they were. Yes, I think you could say they're getting Americanized . . .'

3

Stars and Stripes Over All

THE coming of the American invasion was foreseen by the English upper classes, a sub-group of the human race with exceptional talent for survival, long before most others. They did not resist the inevitable. They invited it into the family bed, marrying off their sons to American heiresses while the class below still prattled of colonials. This historical talent for appeasement had its reward. The invaders handed over their money and were taught manners by the invaded. They thought the bargain good and became more English than the English. The first wave of the American invasion was contained.

It was too late to repeat the technique. Even if there were enough titles and beds to go round the American of the mid-twentieth century no longer needs them. The dollar stands high enough in its own right. The era in which Americans felt it necessary to learn to be Europeans has ended. They are now content that Europeans should learn to be American.

That this is what most Europeans, and indeed the natives of most other continents, want is the premise from which the American invasion starts. So much so, indeed, that not to want to be American is regarded by many Americans as an unfriendly act. A well-known Canadian writer, Hugh MacLennan, who expressed the hope in an article in a popular Canadian magazine that President Kennedy would recognize that some Canadians wished to be Canadian with a Canadian point of view, was publicly rebuked by one of America's best-known columnists for 'as unfriendly an utterance against this country (the United

States) as any I have seen'. His mail was flooded with letters from indignant American citizens asking if Canada was 'turning Cuban or Afro-Asian'. Yet all he had been concerned to say was that it was necessary for Canadians to take thought to preserve their identity. This was, he suggested, in some danger of being extinguished, 'with the best of intentions', by their 'enormous, expansive, good-natured and self-confident' neighbour.

American commercial colonization, rapid and expansive though it is, is, of course, only one aspect of that erosion of Canadian identity of which Mr. MacLennan and others are afraid. What seemed to him even more a matter for concern was the continuous pressure of American culture. Similarly, although the capture of a number of British economic strong points by American finance is important, both for the value these themselves possess and for their influence in fields other than the economic, this economic advance represents only a small part of the American invasion. It now touches in some measure almost every espect of our lives.

Not to expect the culture and way of life of the most powerful and prosperous of the nations of the West to have a forceful impact upon the rest would be unrealistic. That it should do so is a natural part of an historical process which has expressed itself in other forms and through the agency of other nations, including our own, at every stage of civilization.

This American invasion differs, however, from the export of ideas and modes of life which has always characterized international societies in the broad front of its attack and the forces of mass communication upon which it is able to call. Only rarely are these instruments of mass communication used to aid the international interchange of ideas and modes of thought. Their main purpose is to promote a commercialism which is concerned primarily to shape people to the pattern most conforming to the requirements of salesmanship.

The British young get their conceptions of love, courtship, marriage and family life, of dress, social etiquette and professional success from Hollywood equally with the American young – and they are the same for both. Despite some increase in British and Continental films, something like three-quarters of all the feature films shown in British cinemas are American: seven out of ten of those who see them are under the age of thirty-five.

Our television screens sag under American material. Nightly we are bombarded by American Westerns, American crimes series, American comedy films, American show business. American quiz games. No one, sitting through these, is likely to make the mistake of thinking himself privileged by so doing to participate in a flowering of American national culture. He is taking part in a surrender of the will to the conception of society as a captive mass audience, first attracted and then corrupted by the deliberate employment of the most superficial and meretricious modes of entertainment in order to induce a state of acquiescence to the most dishonest and fantastic commercial claims.

That British commercial television should have succumbed so easily to the offerings of its American big brother – although succumbed is scarcely the word, it has rushed headlong to embrace them – is not surprising. Our commercial screens are children of the same interests. It was the immense success of American television as an instrument of salesmanship that provided the power behind the campaign to introduce commercial television here, instead of one of several other possible ways of providing an alternative system to the B.B.C. Without American commercial television independent television in Britain would not have taken the form it did. The American example inspired and shaped it. Those who planned and brought to success one of the most successful pieces of lobbying in British political history – defeating in its course not simply the Labour Opposition but the most respected leaders of the Conservative Party, all of whom were initially against it – were to no small extent able to do so because of the skill, experience and resources of great American advertising agencies and other commercial groups who put their experience behind the campaign.

Commercial television is, in fact, one of America's chief gifts to Britain. We may like it or dislike it – and there is plenty of room for both. We may acknowledge that it sometimes shows

great virtues as well as great defects and that some counter-
balance and corrective to a purely B.B.C. monopoly was necessary, even although it need not have taken this particular form.
We may recognize that the original American model has inevitably been to some extent modified and made, according to
our standards, less obnoxious in response to the character and
pressures of British society. But none of these things should
disguise from us the fact that the idea of selling commercial
television to the British public began as a gleam in the bright
predatory eyes of American advertising agents. They have reason
to feel well satisfied with the result.

So also have the professional providers of American canned
entertainment for the masses. To them British commercial television, ably abetted by a competition-conscious B.B.C., has provided a splendid outlet for second-hand goods. No doubt there
are some bad American television programmes that do not get
exported. But not many. 'British television,' observed Mr. David
Susskind, one of the best of serious American television commentators, on his last visit to London, 'is a refuse heap for the worst
we produce.'

Even when they are permitted to look at something deriving
from their own country British viewers are now often required
to do so through American eyes. An increasing number of the
pre-recorded British films offered to them have been made
primarily for the American market and tailored to give a picture
of Britain satisfying to an American audience.

Even more overwhelmingly American than the programmes
we see on our television screens is the music we hear over the air.
When the British Song Writers Guild made a check over several
weeks of eight of the leading disc jockey programmes on the
B.B.C. they found that even the most British of these eight
programmes carried 67·2 per cent of American records. On the
others the American share of records played ranged from 79 to
91·66 per cent and in the case of one well-known programme was
100 per cent. Over the whole field of recorded music put out by
the B.B.C., both classical and popular, the American share
amounted to 68 per cent.

The sale of records and record players is still booming. The sale of discs alone is now running at close on £1,000,000 a month – more than half to young people under the age of twenty-five. And although there are British idols like Tommy Steele and Adam Faith and Anthony Newly the vast majority of the hit pop records are of American music and American songs.

We watch American. We listen American. We read American. There is scarcely an American best seller written that is not at once published over here – however vapid or meritricious it may be. *Peyton Place* is as real to the suburbs of London or Birmingham as to those of New York or Detroit. Not one word needs to be altered, not one nuance of sex or sentimentality or social gradation changed, to fit them to the British public before they sell in their paper-back thousands on the bookstalls and in the stationer's shops. The American scene has become as real to the British reader as to the American, its values as potent here as there.

Some American publishers would also like to publish our books for us. In November 1960 Heinemann's, one of the largest and most famous of British publishing groups, found itself the centre of a take-over bid by the large American textbook and commercial publishing firm of McGraw Hill. This almost succeeded and might well have done so if the large City interests to which Heinemann's had earlier turned for capital for post-war expansion had not themselves decided that publishing had now become a 'growth industry' susceptible to modern methods of business development and therefore worth keeping. Since then a smaller, but old, established, London publishing firm, W. H. Allen & Co., has been bought by an American publisher. It is unlikely to be the last.

According to Bennett Cerf, head of the American publishing firm of Random House, 1960 was the year Wall Street and American publishing fell in love with each other. The romance produced an unprecedented number of mergers in the New York publishing trade. Wall Street is known to favour making it trans-Atlantic, with profitable 'tie-ups' between American and British publishing houses capable of responding to American commercial methods.

In the expanding field of paper-back publishing American penetration has already gone a good way. The New American Library, one of the largest of the American paper-back publishing houses, owners of Mentor and Signet books, has acquired control of two well-known British paper-back firms, Ace and Four Square. It was subsequently approached by two others but did not buy. Here, as in hard-back publishing, it is not simply the British domestic market that attracts. Whatever our motives and however obscure they must sometimes seem to the student of literature, we still buy more books per head than most other nations. But the Commonwealth market with its appetizing promise of all those millions of Africans and Asians who have still to learn to read – and to read in English – is even more appetizing.

American films, American television programmes, American music, American books. No one but an insular idiot would want to keep them all out. We live by the movement and circulation of ideas. The true American creative artist, whatever his medium, threatens none but the closed of mind and empty of heart. It is not the American writer or actor or singer or film director we need fear – for them there should always be a welcome – but the increasing intrusion of American commercial methods and merchandising exploitation into areas of intellect and culture that need national roots for their support and in which mass appeal ought not to be the only test of value. It is not American art but American admass that threatens us with its concern to turn ideas into no more than handmaidens of commerce.

Not, to be fair, that this American invasion has no interest outside material things. It has its spiritual side. In the United States the combined intelligence of the big advertising agencies when applied to the field of religion in a co-operative campaign has succeeded in making the American people, if not more spiritual, more ready to go to church: attendances have soared since the advertising experts joined in. They have since expressed their willingness, through the American-owned J. Walter Thompson Agency, to do the same for the British people.

Not all churchmen like the idea. However, in the last five

years three American organizations which specialize in teaching religious bodies how to raise funds have opened up business in Britain. All are doing well. More are on the way.

The first to cross the Atlantic was the Wells Organization. Mr. Frank H. Wells, who is in charge of its British operations, is a thirty-year-old Methodist, and grandson of the American founder of the firm. He has demonstrated that what America will take, so too will Britain. Two years after starting here his organization had raised the income of twenty-two British churches from £90,240 to £225,600. By the middle of 1960 he had had pledges totalling £3,000,000 from church parishioners all over the country. His team of salesmen, each of them paid about £2,500 a year, organize training courses for church officials. They teach them public relations, salesmanship and organization. They guarantee results. They have, Mr. Wells feels, done a wonderful job.

The Bishop of Chichester agrees. 'If,' he is quoted as saying, 'commerce possesses certain experience that can be put to good use by the Kingdom of God we ought to draw on what commerce has to offer.' Onward Christian soldiers marching as to war with the gentlemen from Madison Avenue leading on before.

4

Carbon Copy Salvation

ONE cannot assess the full potential effect of the American invasion on the character of British society without looking first at American society and asking how it is standing up in the second half of the twentieth century to the impact of those forces of mass communication and salesmanship which we are already beginning to feel in modified form. Of course much, both good and bad, in American society derives from its own history and is unique and unexportable. But much comes also from economic and social assumptions which, although influenced by that history, have now been given a more universal significance. It is with these we are concerned.

It is, of course, natural enough that America should have a powerful effect on the civilization and culture of the rest of the world. Its size and wealth and still more the energy and resource of its inhabitants, their abounding vitality and confidence in the handling of material things, cannot help but influence others. In the eyes of millions of ordinary people all over the world the American nation represents prosperity for the ordinary man. Not in practice for all ordinary men, although for more than has ever been the case elsewhere, but for the ordinary man as an ideal figure, a symbol of what its nationhood is about. It has given more people a higher standard of living than any nation in the history of the world and has done so in an infinitely shorter space of time than could have been dreamed of when it began.

These 179,000,000 people whose nation has grown in numbers

by 28,000,000 even in the last ten years, and who include within themselves men and women of almost every race, colour and creed under the sun, compose, by reason both of their history and their immense achievements, the matrix of a culture which cannot help but pervade in some degree almost every corner of the earth.

An elderly and distinguished American lady of my acquaintance arrived one evening in Beirut as darkness fell. As she drove from the airport she was entranced by the myriad lights of the modern city flashing their messages across the sky in Arabic: so mysterious, it seemed to her, and so romantic, so promising of strange revelations and new significances. Looking about her out of the window, she clapped her hands and cried, 'But what do they all mean? Tell me, please. What does that one say?' 'It says,' said her Arabian host with grave courtesy, 'it says Coca Cola.' And so it does, that or something else of the same kind, in lights all over the world: America writing its name on the sky for the warning and stimulation of us all.

That American modes should significantly affect our own is to be expected: the United States is the paragon and King Emperor of the industrial civilisation upon which we are all, for good or ill, embarked. To learn and borrow from so powerful and pervasive an exemplar of our times is both natural and inevitable; to learn and borrow from, not to allow oneself to be swamped by.

American society, still so uncertain and so incomplete in so many ways, although so confident and so creative in others, is the product of a unique experience. It carries on its body the scars as well as the triumphs of a Caesarean birth whose pangs are not yet over. Much that it has to offer to the world is capable of enormously enriching the total of human well-being. But much, as has already been remarked, is so largely the outcome of the unique American experience that to seek to graft it on to other and older cultures, born of the slow gestation of centuries and of convolutions of nature and history wholly different from its own, is to lose the most valuable qualities of both.

We are not American. Our countries cannot become American

even should we wish. What we are in danger of becoming as the American invasion gathers force with all its direct and indirect pressures upon us, some of them conscious and deliberate, the attributes and instruments of American economic and merchandising expansion, others less tangible and more innocent yet equally inescapable, a part of the very weather of the streets in which we move, what we are in danger of becoming unless we are careful, is a bastard imitation of a society which is incapable of being wholly recreated in conditions other than its own.

Not, of course, that American society is all of one piece. Chicago is decades away from Boston, the Middle West a different country from New England, the South from both, California – the West generally – a world away from all. No one who knows America even a little would make the mistake of thinking Americans all alike or talk as if it were possible to tie the same label to Vermont and Virginia, Utah, Idaho, Massachusetts, Kentucky and Nevada, Washington, D.C., and Washington State. America is a continent as well as a nation; the flag that symbolizes its unity flies over communities separated not only by the immensity of deserts and mountains and plains but by many habits of behaviour and thought.

Yet although one must always bear this very real diversity in mind, there is nevertheless a genuine sense in which one can talk of a single American civilization, and refer to an American way of life, in terms less subtle than when one refers to European civilization, and more conclusive than when one speaks of an English way of life. No nation in history has ever pinned more faith than this one to the common denominator in the social transaction.

What it is necessary to remember is that the United States is the product of a conformist conscience, and cannot escape from it in any of its affairs. Although Americans like to remind themselves of their non-conformist beginnings, without their basic belief in conformity they could not, in fact, have made themselves into a nation. How else could so immense a merging of peoples and races, English, German, Italian, Irish, Polish, Japanese, Chinese, men and women of almost every country under the sun, have shed so wholly their past inheritance and taken on a new personality: the personality of an American? Never has a country been required to accelerate to such an extent as this one the historical processes of assimilation, create synthetically, in so brief a span of time, a new human species.

Only the conformist conscience made it possible; the conviction that there is something admirable in being alike, in a oneness of national personality capable of transcending all the differences of individual interest and attitude and heritage. Conformism has been the essential ingredient of American survival: the mortar that alone could bind together people so different, and erect, in this country of vast spaces, containing within itself every conceivable variety of climate and scenery and natural resource, out of human material so diverse, a strong and unshakeable edifice of nationality.

No person of imagination can help but be moved by the magnitude and durability of the achievement. Yet the very qualities which were required to make it possible and which hold it together make this civilization the least suitable of almost any for universal imitation.

Many Americans find this suggestion wounding. They feel themselves personally involved in every aspect of their social system. They built it with their own hands, or if they did not do so their fathers or grandfathers did. It must be perfect because they made it. Not to admire it and wish to copy it is therefore to reject them.

Shortly after the war, a group of young people from all the Marshall Aid countries were chosen, after the requisite amount of essay writing and interviewing, to visit the United States as the guests of the *New York Herald Tribune* and take part in an international youth forum. They were treated with superb hospitality. They were taken to the White House to meet President Truman, and to the F.B.I. to be introduced to Mr. J. Edgar Hoover. They were conducted over an automobile plant in Detroit and flown down to Texas, where they were each given a ten-gallon hat, and to Los Angeles, where they met Mr. Disney. And as one of the most valuable parts of their visit each stayed for some weeks at the home of an American boy or girl and was introduced to American teen-age life in all its plenitude – so different from the war-time austerities or actual deprivations in which their own childhood had been spent. The mothers and fathers of the American boys and girls with whom they stayed could not do too much for them. The warm, generous American heart went out to meet them with all the loving hospitality of which it is so abundantly capable. They had a wonderful time.

When the day came for them to leave, their hosts almost invariably asked: 'Don't you wish you could stay? Wouldn't you love to live in America?'

When these children from Europe replied with grave courtesy that they had had the time of their lives and had enjoyed every minute of it, but although they loved America it was their own countries they wanted to live in, many of these parents were deeply hurt. To some of them, I was told later, it seemed like a slap in the face. Not to want to live in America! How could they be so ungrateful – how so rejecting?

Many visitors to America must similarly remember occasions on which they were met by blank incredulity from waitresses, taxi-drivers and others when they explained courteously that much as they liked America they were looking forward to going home. This is not because Americans mind criticism. Indeed they enjoy it and often do their best to incite it. They like to take their society apart and scrutinize it. They find pleasure in being harder on their institutions than many of them deserve and in attributing corruption in public life even where it does not exist. They often seem to find satisfaction in comparing to their disadvantage particular aspects of their way of running things with what is done in Britain or elsewhere.

But none of this shakes their deep conviction that not only is American civilization the greatest in the world but that other countries both wish and ought to wish to have it. The differences between national cultures seem to them (I do not, of course, speak here of the intelligent and sophisticated minority but of the broad mass of ordinary Americans in so far as a visitor can get to know them) not to be a valuable expression of human variety but a confession either of failure in energy or of positive wrong-headedness – perhaps even of downright wickedness – on the part of those who follow non-American ways, especially when then have been given a chance to know better.

The Americans are men and women who have found the good news – that after all is what the whole American experiment has been about. They must cry aloud salvation. They cannot believe that if the word is shown to the world, the world – except of course for Communists,who are by definition evil – will not accept it. This is even truer of the new Americans than the old, for to them the choice is closer and even more a part of their own personal affirmation. Moreover, living, as so many do, pulled first this way and then that by the old life and the new, they need the constant reassurance that they were right in making the choice they did.

Nothing is more remarkable in American life than the almost compulsive rejection by the children of many first generation immigrants of the language, ways and manners of their parents – and the proud and willing acceptance of this rejection by the parents themselves. They see in it a confirmation not only of their own decision but of their brightest hopes. Held back by the past, they know, sadly, that they themselves cannot expect ever wholly to make the great change, But their children can. They, at least, can become American. What is a parental heartbreak to set in the balance against that?

The impact of American culture on the rest of the world has often, in consequence of all this, something of the force of a compulsive neurosis; to question any part of it is to set one's face against the light. Moreover, the speed and ruthlessness of the Americans' conquest of nature in the vast territory over which they have spread themselves, balanced by an equal ruthlessness in dealing with such native inhabitants as stood in their path, have left them, for the most part, impatient or un-understanding of the ecology of human communities – the interdependence of man and his environment, the delicate balance of past and present in the evolution of society. Their instinct is to build the world anew and not bother about local susceptibilities.

This single-mindedness sometimes makes them unpopular in backward areas with no great taste for civilization and less for hygiene. But it lends to the American invasion elsewhere something of the power of a force of nature. This is especially so because the American invasion is much less one of philosophy than of methods and products, and American refrigerators are on the whole less easy to refute than American ideas. The American firms which are now entering British and other markets in increasing numbers are doing something much more effective than preaching a way of life — they are selling one.

It is the variety and volume of American consumption that most marks it out from all other nations in the world. In no other society does the ordinary man – and still more the ordinary woman – buy so much. It is probably impossible for any other society to reach a similar level of consumption without turning itself into a carbon copy of America to whatever extent its economic resources allow.

The level of American consumption is not something imposed on American society – a rich icing on a cake not otherwise very different from others. It is an integral part of the American culture, a built-in response to needs deriving from the nature of American history, a potent force in shaping the present and future of this society.

Of course the rest of the world can learn much from what America has to offer. But as the American invasion proceeds on its seemingly inexorable way, backed by all the authority of American technological achievement and the power of American merchandising know-how, and driven onwards by the deep American need to be assured that the society it has created is an admired exemplar for others, it is important that we who are being invaded should take a long, clear look at American society and try to separate the myth from the reality.

The whole cloth of American society may suit the majority of Americans admirably – although that is not so certain as it once seemed. It could become a winding sheet, and not a very well-fitting one at that, for a culture, such as our own.

Let us, therefore, before looking further into the extent of the American invasion of Britain so far, and the still greater invasion that almost certainly lies ahead, take a long look at what the methods we are now being asked to welcome have done to American society itself.

Unless we take care, that is the shape of our future.

5

Only the Needy Need Cash

IN the last ten years the suburban population of the United States has grown by 81 per cent. Everywhere the real estate developments proliferate: a vast urban sprawl stretching out from New York, Washington, Chicago, Philadelphia, San Francisco, Los Angeles, Seattle, Houston, Phoenix, and every other city; unplanned, uncontrolled, unco-ordinated – there are 1,467 different governing bodies in the greater New York area alone for a population of about 15,000,000, an average of one governing body to every 10,000 people.

They spread out from the cities for mile after mile, these new suburban dwellings, flung as by some vast impersonal force on each side of the great freeways that cut across the countryside like scars from the knife of a demonic giant.

Along the freeways the automobiles move with the smooth unbroken power of black water over a mill race (the swish, swish, swish, swish of their tyres on the concrete is like the steady roar from the pool below). Swiftly, implacably they travel, three or four abreast, at sixty-five miles an hour, each the same distance behind another in its appointed lane so that to move from one lane to another is a matter of the most extreme difficulty. One must position oneself miles ahead to be sure of being at the right place at the right time for the right turn-off in order to avoid being carried on another fifteen or twenty miles before it is possible to escape – but to the wrong suburb.

Alongside the freeways the used car lots flash by, the gas

stations, the drive-ins, the motels, the restaurants, the liquor
stores, Jack's Inn, Meg's Place, Hot Dogs, Hamburgers, Steaks,
Jumbo Eats, Al's Nook: desolating and tawdry. From each
vacant lot the gigantic bill boards howl aloud the news that the
American milleniium is already here and the automobiles in their
thousands race unseeingly past, homing without pause, like
creatures of a new civilization born with rubber tyres in place
of feet, to the comforting embrace of the suburban paradises
beside the turn-offs and clover leafs, the under passes and the
over passes.

It is the suburbs, at once social and rootless, their blood cor-
puscles the automobiles, their spiritual heart the gleaming all-
comprehensive shopping centres, their dominant personality
feminine – it is the suburbs, so ugly and anonymous in their mass
impact yet so architecturally pleasant in their individual houses,
that most express the modern face of America. It is here that the
civilization that America has for export is most to be found. This
is what America in the twentieth century is about, this is what
all those big American executives sent to run British businesses
have as the vision ahead.

Not all the suburbs are the same of course. There are rich
suburbs, middle-class suburbs, cheap suburbs, suburbs for those
who have reached the top and suburbs for those who are on their
way up with eyes on the still grander suburbs with a 'nicer'
kind of people to which one day they will move. Nor, of course,
do all Americans live in suburbs even yet. There are still towns
which have been there for a long time and which, though they
have changed and developed, remain very much themselves
with recognizable identities different from those of others: like
Berkeley in which my wife and I lived during our most recent
stay in America, or those still older townships in the East with
their social distinctions as rigid as any in Europe, or the more
open but equally rooted townships of the Middle West which
often look so alike that it is is difficult to tell one from the other.

But although not all Americans live in suburbs the suburban
population is spiralling higher and higher each year. Already
two thirds of the entire population lives in urban areas – and a

much greater proportion of the young married population. Each year 33,000,000 Americans move into a new neighbourhood. Each year the suburbs spread farther and farther. In California, for instance, where the population is increasing by birth and migration at the rate of one a minute, and which, because of its attraction for so many Americans from so many other parts of this vast continent, represents to a greater degree than any other State the shape of the future, it is calculated that at the present rate of expansion the suburbs may spread without break almost every inch of the 400 miles from San Francisco to Los Angeles in another fifteen years.

The ranch-style houses and garden apartments, the 'luxurious split-level homes' and colonial-style mansions with their Living Forums and Sleeping Chambers, patios, play decks and barbecue pits, their sun-rooms, 'bi-level brunch bars', mud rooms, 'massive chimney blocks' and two car ports, enfold in gracious living the American century. They offer all – or almost all – that twentieth-century man has a right to hope for. Even his spiritual well-being is not overlooked. In California one can buy a split level, four-bedroom house with 'a tiny chapel (shaped like a cross) right in the middle of one's home for those many Americans disillusioned by a completely material life'. The space can, the brochure adds cagily, be utilized as 'a sewing alcove for her or a den for him' by those who do not happen to need a chapel.

What kind of life do the people who inhabit these dream houses with their open-living plans, their picture windows and their gleaming kitchens with the automatic cookers, and dish washers, electric mixers and deep freezes, live?

Despite the unemployment endemic to the American system – odd how so little concerned so warmhearted a people can manage to be about the five millions of their fellow countrymen for whom all this industrial efficiency cannot find a job – and the fact that a third of all American families are still, according to the last census, living on incomes below the comfort line, the way of life for most is extraordinarily prosperous. Each year it gets more so. Over the last ten years the typical American family income has risen by 63 per cent and there can be few in these

raw, expanding suburbs who are not a good deal better off today
than ever they were before.

Yet most live constantly in debt.

Naturally, the new house in the suburbs is bought on mortgage.
That would be equally true in England, or France or Scandinavia.
But the initial capital payment is likely to be much smaller.
'City-Close, Country-Quiet', scream the huge advertisements,
'Four-bedroom, 2-bath homes from $14,495 ... Thermostatically
controlled heat ... sliding glass doors ... built-in range, oven,
and ventilating hood ... wall to wall carpet ... glass enclosed
shower in master bath ... garbage disposer ... acoustical type
ceilings ... double sinks ... flooring, walls, wallpaper, wainscot,
counter-top all colour-co-ordinated ... MOVE IN FOR $395.
And a mile or two down the freeway ' U Pay Only $100. No
Deposit for Veterans'.

Even those whose aspirations turn to life in 'a mushrooming,
self-contained residential community for executive-type buyers
where the price range is in keeping with a high-class residential
project' ($32,950 to $49,500 for a ranch-style house with three
bedrooms and two bathrooms, $72,500 to $85,000 for something
a little grander with a Japanese Shinto fountain at the entrance)
need not repine that their executive careers have so far allowed
them to do so little saving: 'All credit facilities available'.

Where, however, the American suburban dweller most differs
from his British counterpart is not in the fact that he will have a
bigger mortgage, but that he is also very likely to be in debt
for almost everything else. In suburbia everything is free – only
the future is mortgaged. 'On the cuff, go-now, buy-now, live-
now, pay-later' is the magic slogan of the age.

Without credit the suburbs could not exist. Their prosperity
floats on a sea of debt. According to evidence given before a
Senate Committee under Senator Paul Douglas in 1960 personal
debts in America have quadrupled in the last twenty years. They
now amount to only a little short of $200,000,000,000 or just
over £70,000,000,000. This sum is owed on credit, mortgage,
and hire-purchase agreements by some one hundred million
people. It is estimated that in the next ten years the debt for

consumer credit, apart altogether from house mortgages, will double again.

Never in the history of mankind have so many owed so much for so many things. Indeed, if Americans were now to stop spending what they have not got their whole economy would falter. It is only by mortgaging their futures they avoid bank-ruptcy. Thrift, so highly regarded by an earlier generation of Americans, has become a dirty word. Not to live beyond your immediate means is anti-social, a rejection of the spending philosophy which has made America what it now is.

In America these days the problem is not how to borrow but how to avoid doing so. On one short drive through the main street of Gertrude Stein's home town, Oakland, California, I passed the offices of ten loan agencies all offering me money in neon lights: to borrow is to borrow is to borrow. One of the plushiest Sunday evening television programmes on the West Coast is sponsored by a money-lender. Everywhere there is the invitation to plunge into debt.

Two-thirds of all the new motor-cars sold, half the furniture, more than half the television sets, dishwashers, washing machines, deep freezes, electric mixers, outboard motor-boats, Wurlitzer organs and the rest of the concomitants of twentieth-century American civilization would not be sold if there were a pause in the credit expansion. Mail-order sales on up to twenty-four months' credit have more than doubled since 1950.

Nor is it only for such tangible, if constantly wasting, assets that Americans borrow. Life depends on debt.

'Babies are being born on the instalment plan,' writes Mr. Hillel Black, one of the most thorough of recent investigators into this golden field of personal credit in a recently published study, *Buy Now, Pay Later*. 'Children go through college on time, even funerals are being paid for on what the English quaintly call the never never. Through debt people are buying hairpins, toothpaste, mink coats, girdles, tickets to baseball games, religious medallions, hi-fi equipment, safaris in Africa . . .' It is, in fact, almost impossible to think of anything in this lush, and, to the innocent observer, staggeringly prosperous American way of life, that cannot be bought on credit, from having the kitchen made over or the front yard landscaped, to an evening at a restaurant with a night club to follow; from a do-it-yourself kit to contact lenses or a 'Disaster Shelter – $295 complete; terms.'

In interest on personal loans Americans now pay more than half as much again as the total interest on the whole of the Federal Debt. 'Nothing Down! Months to Pay!' 'Buy What You Want, When You Want It!' plead the store advertisements: it is not so much an advertising slogan as a philosophy of living. To carry money in your pocket has become a sign of failure: only the needy need cash. If you are successful you have a credit card. For six dollars down you can charge for your gasolene and your motel bills, your lunch, your theatre trip, your vacation abroad, a summer outfit and a hair-do for your wife, port wine colour casuals and a cream sports jacket for yourself. You are translated on the flip of a credit card into the legendary millionaire too rich to bother with loose change.

To the Englishman, the Frenchman, the German or the Scandinavian the negotiation of a small bank loan may still, despite some recent overtures by the banks themselves, be a matter for caution and trepidation. Not so in the United States. Here, banks long to be visited. So much so in fact that, as *Life* recently recorded, one bank in Arizona has taken to giving teas and carillon concerts to attract clients. Several others offer housewives free lessons in home dressmaking and the laying of tile floors. One bank in New York floods its central lobby and puts on an ice show at Christmas to bring the customers in.

But of course they must not simply be brought in. They must stay to borrow. This is where the latest and perhaps greatest of banking inventions comes in: 'Instant Money'. Although the idea of Instant Money (after all if Instant Coffee why not Instant Money too!) only came to its inventor, the First National Bank of Boston, at the end of 1955, close on two hundred banks all over the States now use it and a Bankers' Convention was recently warned – or rather encouragingly advised – that in time it may well replace every other means of household buying apart from the open charge account with the neighbourhood grocer.

To use Instant Money you do not need to have an account with a bank or deposit any money with it. You walk in and join the bank as a borrower from the word go and are provided with a book of 'Instant Checks' differing from ordinary cheques only in their colour. You then use these Instant Checks to the agreed amount just as if you actually had money at the bank.

Naturally, since banks after all must live, you pay a monthly instalment covering capital and interest against your loan. But you need never pay it all off. On the contrary, the principle which has made Instant Money so successful is that of revolving credit. As the loan is reduced by each monthly instalment the credit on which the client can draw is simultaneously increased by the same amount. He and the bank are together for keeps.

'We have found,' proudly declared a Vice-President of the Citizens and Southern National Bank of Atlanta after introducing Instant Money, 'an entirely new market for lending funds in our bank. Those who use it,' he added appreciatively, 'find it a painless method of stretching their budget during the painful times, an easy, convenient, dignified way to pick up the cash necessary to enjoy the flexibility in their budget which they must have in order to live a satisfying life.'

Credit, credit and yet more credit. And since Americans believe so much in youth it would obviously be wrong to shut the young out of the golden dream. If you are old enough to date you are old enough to borrow. A survey made by *Seventeen Magazine* in 1960 showed that of the 217 large stores covered by its investigation 64 per cent ran credit schemes for teen-agers, double the percentage disclosed in a survey a year earlier. Since the 'market potential' of American teen-agers is estimated to be close on $10,000,000 a year and is expected to be twice this within another five or six years, to teach children how to buy the American way is clearly good business. Besides, in the young, habits are important. As the Merchandise Director of *Seventeen* told the Credit Management Division of the National Retail Merchants Association: 'It is easier to start a habit than to stop one, so start the credit habit in your store with your young customers.'

To promote this habit the co-operation of the schools is being invited – it is after all their function to make Americans. High Schools in more than 1,300 cities are now using a fifty-four page booklet with coloured illustrations on how to use credit, produced by the National Foundation for Consumer Credit. Local boards of education have in some cases arranged for High Schools and Junior High Schools to visit stores for 'laboratory lessons'.

One forward-looking merchant has actually established an 'honour' system with the approval of the local school authorities and the Parent-Teachers Association. Under this engaging scheme the boy or girl starts off with a white 'honour card' allowing up to $25 to be spent on credit, moves on from this to a silver honour card raising the level by another $10 and finally – having shown themselves energetic borrowers although young – to the final accolade of a golden honour credit card raising the credit limit to $50.

In the survey made by the magazine *Seventeen* several stores were able to claim that they already had between 500 and 1,000 teen-age boys and girls on their credit lists. One had more than 1,400.

One result of easy credit all round is that a great many Americans have ceased to be interested in the actual cost of what they buy. They are concerned only with Budgetism – that great American principle described by *Fortune* as the 'Opiate of the Middle Class'. The test of buying, in other words, is not what an article costs – a piece of kitchen equipment, new furniture, a packaged vacation trip – but how the credit payments on it can be fitted into a weekly or monthly budget already heavily loaded with debt. If the merchant selling the article can offer credit terms that will fit into this budget that is all that matters. According to the evidence of marketing and other surveys fewer and fewer customers, and in particular fewer and fewer young middle-class married customers, are now interested in the price of the long-term goods they buy. Nor, for that matter, in the total amount of interest they are letting themselves in for over the years.

Many retailers now make considerably more profit out of the

interest on credit financing than on the sale of the actual goods. Moreover, with the rapid development of 'Peace of mind' insurance, any residual anxiety they may once have had about finding themselves left with a burden of bad debts has gone. Since its invention 'Peace of mind' insurance has reached a total of over $30,000,000,000. The number of policies has increased by 2,000 per cent in the last ten years alone.

'Peace of mind insurance' means that the store from which you buy, shall we say, a new washer or a colour television set sells you at the same time a credit life insurance policy. The premiums are added to the monthly credit payment on the washer or television and the policy covers any credit outstanding if you die. The money goes direct to the store, which is thus relieved of any need to try to get it from your bereaved family.

With 'Peace of mind' credit insurance policies to cover all your credit payments – they already cover well over half the consumer debt in the United States – and a safe job in a big corporation, there is really nothing more for you to worry about (so long, that is, as you believe that there cannot possibly be any serious break in American prosperity and that even if there is so large a part of the population is up to its neck in debt that the Government would have to do something to save it from itself). And there is even less reason than before to concern yourself about the actual cost of anything.

This not only suits the merchant, who can now sell luxury-priced goods to millions of people who cannot afford them and would never have bought them in the days when they still asked what things cost. It also suits the manufacturer, who is not only thus assured of a constantly expanding market for what he makes but also need no longer try to produce down to a price as he formerly had to do. Indeed, American manufacturing and selling for the domestic market is now so integrated with large-scale credit buying, and depends so largely upon it, that any really successful invasion of other countries must almost certainly require that they are persuaded to buy in the same way. This is why American firms in Britain are spending so much money developing new sales techniques under the supervision of American executives.

To be fair, although the system means that everyone pays far more for what they buy than they formerly did, or than they would need to do if they bought for cash – but after all one must expect to pay for 'living graciously' and getting one's pleasures before one has actually earned them – the lessening of the compulsion to manufacture down to a price has had a stimulating effect on the design of many household goods. It accounts in part, no doubt, for the superiority of most American domestic equipment over British in so many small but tantalizing ways.

The British electric oven of the 'very newest design' in which the hot cupboard and the grilling compartment have to double for each other, so that if you are grilling you have nowhere to keep dishes and plates warm and if you are not grilling but roasting you must take out a large and heavy grilling pan and find somewhere to lay it down before you can put your dishes to warm; the oven in another 1962 British model, which instead of being one unit which can be lifted out complete for cleaning, allows you only to remove the sides on the somewhat revolting theory that any grease that splashes on the top will burn off anyway; the dishwasher which does not, as even the oldest American models do, let steam escape or open automatically to release it when the washing process is over so that the dishes will dry more quickly; the coffee percolators which cannot be immersed in water for washing because the elements are exposed; the pop-up toasters so much larger and more clumsy than the American ones; all these and a score of other irritating differences must, one presumes – or at least it is charitable to suppose so – be due, not to any basic inferiority on the part of British designers, but to the fact that they have to think much more about manufacturing down to a price than the Americans do, and must therefore 'cut out the frills' or make one component do the work of two.

Unhampered by the same compulsion the American manufacturer can design and make equipment that is thought-out as a complete unit capable of performing easily and efficiently all the functions that are likely to be expected of it and that also looks attractive. He knows that if he does so it will sell, even though the cost is more than it would otherwise be, so long as credit terms can be arranged that will fit into a middle-class American budget. Capital cost is not important. It is the monthly or weekly payment that counts.

Budgetism also accounts for another aspect of American household buying that differs a good deal from ours. This is the much greater price competition in foodstuffs and other articles of regular household consumption. American domestic budgets are so loaded, the fixed charges on the salary cheque are so great, the proportion of free income relatively so small, that ordinary weekly household buying of food and so on must also be rigorously fitted into the prevailing budgetism. Hence the constant price-cutting offers (Prime lamb chops 5 cents a pound cheaper, Friday: all canned soups down 6 cents) advertised so lavishly in press and radio and studied so carefully by the housewife before she sets out in her car to do the weekly shopping. In this field, where credit does not operate, price counts and counts a lot.

Only the very rich can afford to pay more than they need when it is a matter of cash. Only they can afford to pay less than the rest when it is a matter of credit.

For the majority of young Americans the bill for 'living graciously' is high. But why worry? You don't have to pay it *now*.

If you think this is a dangerous way of going on walk round a new housing estate near London before you start criticising the Americans and ask yourself how much of what is inside is now being bought in the same way.

We are not up to the Americans yet. But the hire purchase debt in Britain has reached £900,000,000, and it is rising every year.

6

Two Gallons of Ice Cream

THE immense American enthusiam for buying on credit comes in part, from a demonstration of status – the man who has credit not only shows that he believes in himself but that others do. Most British families who buy through hire purchase still keep quiet about it. Not so in America. There, to buy on credit is different from owing money. Semantically at least. And in America it is semantics that count.

But that $200,000,000,000 of consumer credit is also a demonstration that for Americans the world really is golden, that things will get better and better and better and that what you want you can have now. 'We are shifting,' says Dr.Ernest Dicher, President of the Institute of Motivational Research, 'from a puritanical to a hedonistic age. We are more concerned with immediate happiness than counting on delayed satisfactions in life, or the life hereafter. A credit card is a symbol of this age. We are getting our pleasures, our entertainments, before we have actually earned them.'

It does not, of course, always quite work out like that. Sometimes it proves easy to spend, more difficult to pay. To meet such eventualities several of the credit organizations and collection agencies employ psychologists to advise them on how best to get their money.

Their advice is to induce anxiety tempered with hope. The collection agency, says Dr. Timothy Costello, a Professor of Psychology at New York University, must arouse both 'a positive friendly feeling and anxiety' – it must frighten the client into paying, but not frighten him so much that he will stop buying on credit in the future or go for his credit elsewhere.

One of the most successful methods of doing so is that embodied in a letter approved by the National Retail Credit Association. 'A good credit standing is a priceless asset,' recipients are reminded, 'don't allow delay in your instalments to dull your fine credit record.' He who steals my purse steals trash but he who filches from me my credit card leaves me poor indeed.

Another method found useful by some is to remind the creditor that a parent with a bad credit card may well jeopardize not only his own but his children's chance of credit. No American parent wishes to be the one to snatch the golden honour card out of his infant's hands. Nor need he do so. One's means may be mortgaged years ahead but there is plenty more credit to pay what is already owing.

In a *Fortune* survey a typical middle-income family with an annual salary of $6,000 was cited. Each month the husband, a cost accountant, receives a paycheck of $416 net. When fixed charges, including mortgage payments, car payments, furniture instalments, instalments on a loan for medical expenses, and payment on a revolving credit plan at a department store are met, and food and lunches looked after, there is $45 left for the month to cover clothing, cleaning, laundry, baby-sitting, entertainment and everything else: 'There will not be enough money. But no matter, the deficit can easily be taken care of by another loan.'

Suburbia, as Mr. Hillel Black points out in the brilliant survey already quoted, demands of such families as this a standard of life which they want desperately but could not afford without credit. Moreover, as they move up in the suburban social scale, they will constantly have to seek out more debt: 'Whenever they catch up with the Joneses the Joneses always re-finance.'

Despite the pressures, most suburban families manage, if only by constant reborrowing, to keep up their credit payments. Not to do so would be to abdicate from civilization.

The fact that they do so does not, the credit psychologists

consider, mean that honesty is a usual human trait. It simply means that most Americans have been subject to the proper conditioning.

No doubt the English can be conditioned in the same way. The American firms now flooding into the British consumer market certainly think so. But we shall all have to help.

'Prompt payment of debts among the majority of people,' a leading member of the group of American former university psychologists now devoting themselves to helping their employers to get the money in, told the National Retail Merchants' Association, 'is the result of a complex process of social conditioning involving parental teaching, social pressures, vague feelings of legal consequences and so on. The fact that such a large proportion of people do pay their bills attests to the success of this social conditioning.'

However, even in the United States there is another side.

Those whose social conditioning has been inadequate – or who find themselves faced in the end with a load of debt they no longer feel able to meet – can, in all but four States, have their wages commandeered by legal process and deductions made at source under a garnishment order. Such orders tend to be brought in the main against those in the lower-income groups. But they are far from being exceptional. When the Credit Union National Association surveyed the situation in four cities, including Washington, D.C., and San Francisco, a few years ago, it found that the total number of garnishments in these four cities in the previous twelve months numbered 85,000. And testimony before a Senate Committee on consumer credit disclosed that in a number of cases the issue of a garnishment order against an employee brought instant dismissal by his employers. In one such case a woman with twenty-five years' service was sacked without appeal because her son, for whom she had co-signed a credit agreement, had fallen behind in his instalments. To blaspheme against the law of credit is a dangerous business for Americans.

Testifying before this same Senate Committee, the Chairman of the Committee for Fair Practices in Illinois referred bitterly to 'the human suffering, the break-up of families, the breakdown of individual morale, the deprivation of the very necessities of life' which had resulted on several occasions within his own experience from 'so-called easy-payment plans which wound up being very difficult indeed'. So difficult in fact do buy-now-pay-later agreements turn out in some cases that in the past ten years the number of family bankruptcies in the United States has trebled. It is now, despite the great increase in the general level of family incomes in the interval, higher than at the worst period of the great depression of the 'thirties.

This is the debit side of the great American consumer civilization.

Yet despite the casualties among the lower-income groups – those groups for whom American society shows such little concern in all matters – it would be wrong to imagine that credit buying on so vast a scale is felt to be dangerous by the majority of Americans. On the contrary this is how they want it. Only so can the immense American hunger for material things which is now being transmitted with such verve to our own and other societies be satisfied. If we want to buy like Americans we must first learn to borrow like Americans.

In American society the need to buy takes precedence over almost all other emotions – even that of sex, much as Americans dwell on this in their literature. At once romantic and pathetic, the urge to buy and buy again is at the heart of the American dream. To buy and to waste.

In this society, so recently yet so tremendously removed from the struggles of the pioneers and the anxieties and hardships of the new immigrants, conspicuous expenditure would appear to represent an essential release of the national spirit and conspicuous waste in eating, buying and living a compulsive rejection of the frugalities of the past.

Only so, surely, to take one example, can the huge, and to a European taste, physically nauseating prodigality of the meals served in American popular restaurants be explained. No one can actually wish to eat all those immense steaks, those vast chops, those enormous piles of tasteless jumbo prawns, those salads garnished with so strident a mixture of sauces that the palate falters. Indeed, in many popular restaurants the managements

make evident their awareness that no one can actually consume all that custom demands shall be put on their plates.
They offer you a greaseproof paper bag to take the leavings
home in for your dog – if you happen to have a dog. (In the
better establishments these bags are embellished with pictures of
the sort of dog you would be likely to meet at a Dog Toggery
on Fifth Avenue.)

To serve such helpings, to offer deliberately more than the
most gluttonous can want, to insist on waste as part of the social
garnishing of a meal, this one suspects is a necessary ritualistic
gesture, like the vast meals served in the desert by Arab hosts or
the blow-out of a poor man celebrating a lucky day at the races.

Only in their provision of cutlery do the Americans reveal
the subconscious hold on them of ancestral memories of a more
frugal past. That a people so unnecessarily lavish in all else – and
with so many electric dishwashers – should, except in the most
expensive restaurants and sophisticated households, regard one
knife as adequate for all the requirements of civilized eating is
incomprehensible except on the thesis of an ancestral memory
bogged down in frugal recollections of how hard cutlery was
to come by in a frontier camp. In the same way the inability of a
people otherwise so technically adroit to master the simple rules
for making tea can only, surely, be explained on the basis of a
psychological blockage in the Bostonian memory.

To buy largely and extravagantly has become a necessary
expression of American personality; to have what one wants now
when one wants it, hardly less so. But what one wants must be
wanted by other people also. It must have a symbolic and a
group value as well as a personal and practical one. It is necessary
to be able to buy now to show that one is rich – as a child or a
millionaire is rich, without thought of the future. But also to
show that one belongs.

It is on this passionate conviction of so many Americans – not
all of course, but enough, more than enough – that to buy is to
grow in personality, that the whole vast edifice of American
merchandising and selling is founded. Whatever else American
civilization may mean – and of course it means many other

things, including many that are fine and generous and uplifting to the human spirit – it means, that all who participate in it must face the constant command to buy more and more. If we opt for an Anglicized version of the American way of life we must opt for this also.

In the service of that command the American advertising industry spends on behalf of national advertisers something over $4,000,000,000 a year (roughly £1,400,000,000, or about one-and-a-half times as much as the total annual public bill for all education, including university education, in the United Kingdom). Moreover, in addition to national advertising the American consumer is daily subjected, to an extent far beyond that known elsewhere, to a constant outpouring of local advertising by merchandising firms of all kinds. Many local newspapers receive 60 per cent or more of their total advertising revenue from such sources and are as a result able to function on daily circulations, sometimes of 10,000 copies or less, which would be derisory in Britain.

And all the time the pleading, commanding voices swell in an ever larger chorus from local radio and television stations, on bill-boards and circulars. When all the channels of American national and local advertising are taken into account at least $10,000 a minute is spent every hour of the twenty-four, every day of the week, every week of the year persuading Americans to buy. It may well be more.

By night and by day the air is full of voices. For radio, which goes on practically non-stop throughout the twenty-four hours, is still important in American advertising because of the number of car radios and of housewives who listen as they do their daily chores. These voices are full of a passion, a raucousness, a treacly sentimentality, a glad-hand buttonholing matey-ness, a vulgarity and a mendacity almost impossible to believe.

There is nothing they do not try to sell, these wheedling, bellowing, crooning voices of a civilization which, if they were all one had to judge by, would seem to have lost all sense of honesty or respect for human dignity: toilet tissues, diapers, loans, new cars, second-hand cars, furniture, steaks, washing powder, cat food, banking services, dentures ('You pay as you chew'), hi-fi records, religion, soft toys, soft drinks, cremation ('call on B. your *friendly* mortician today folks and find that peace of mind you're looking for'), refrigerators, deep freeze, frying-pans, toasters, cold curers, lamb chops, deodorants ('When it's winter outside remember it's summer under your arm-pits'), hair-do's, corn cures, insurance, breakfast foods, shorts, suspenders, personalized tie tacks, potato chips, towels for him, towels for her, cut-price groceries, hardware, gasolene, drapes, silverware, houses, canned goods, beer — on and on, day in day out, night in night out, shouted, whispered, sung, acted; punctuated by drum beats, bugle blasts, ticker-tapes, children singing, children crying, women cajoling, men laughing; by whispers of love, of desire, of hope, of longing, of despair: an endless, gluttonous outpouring of synthetic emotion winging its way for ever and ever across the plains and mountains, the cities and towns, the freeways and homesteads of this immense country.

But do not mock. The political and commercial pressures for commercial radio in Britain are mounting daily. For forty years British listeners have been content with public service regional broadcasting. Even when the decision on commercial television was taken there was no serious suggestion that the principle should be extended to sound radio. It is scarcely accidental that it is only now as the pressures to Americanize British buying habits increase with every fresh inroad of American capital and American sales techniques that a campaign for local commercial radio stations should have been launched, backed by powerful advertising and newspaper interests including some, like Thomson newspapers, with trans-Atlantic experience.

In the daytime and half-way through the night the television screens take up the American story with an even more frenetic and expensive gusto. No question of natural breaks here, every man and woman's shoulder is to the wheel. The singers, the quiz masters, the comedians, the stars and starlets, even the newscasters and the commentators on world affairs, must pause in their activities to tell you confidentially what their sponsor has to sell. ('And now, folks, turning aside from Berlin for one moment – but we'll be taking another look at how things are with the latest stop press flash before this programme ends – let me pass on to you some news that's really worth knowing, news that means money in all your pockets . . .') History, tragedy, music, humour, ballet, political reporting, all are impressed in the service of a common master – all must be dedicated to the all-pervasive religion of the soft or the hard sell.

One can, of course, turn off the television and the radio. But in the morning and evening come the newspapers – immense, diffuse, swollen in size almost beyond the ability to handle with their pages and pages and pages of advertisements. The telephone rings. 'Can you tell me,' says a golden voice, 'what is the name of the President who's head appears on a ten-dollar bill.' 'I'm sorry I can't. I'm English, I've never noticed.' 'You English! Well isn't that just wonderful. Gee I just love the way you folks speak. Who was the President who was born in a log cabin?' 'Well now, more than one I should say. Lincoln maybe and Garfield.' 'Gee isn't that just swell. You English certainly are taught history good. This is the Greenbaum Foto Studio Friday Quiz and your prize is a beautiful cabinet-size portrait of yourself or your wife. Your folks back home will think that's swell I know. Mr. Greenbaum will call you in just one hour and fix everything. You'll surely like that portrait. And all you need to do is to order six others to get that cabinet-size portrait specially mounted free. Just fancy you knowing all about our Presidents. I must tell my mom about that . . .' 'No thank you, I don't want any portraits.' 'But you won one. I asked you which President . . .' 'No, I'm sorry.' 'Well isn't that too bad. Say, you just think it over and ring me back. I'll be here. It's certainly been a pleasure talking to you. It surely has . . .'

There is a ring at the door.

The bright, efficient young man with the large smile and the neat grey suit seizes your hand and shakes it enthusiastically.

'Well, sir,' he says, 'this is indeed a pleasure. I am delighted to meet you. Mr. White was most emphatic that I must call on you right away. "Whatever you do," he said, "don't you miss out on that." ' 'Mr. White?' 'Mr. Lindley J. White. Mr. White wanted

you to be one of the very first to have the news.' 'The news?'
'You've said it, sir. Great news. This is news you're going to be
thrilled to hear. The Quiet Heart Garden of Rest has bought a
whole new section of wonderful, peaceful, restful landscape . . .'
'I'm sorry. I'm English. I . . .' 'You're English, well now isn't
that wonderful. Why, I just can't wait to tell Mr. White. Why,
only this morning Mr. White said to me, "Herman," he said,
"what I aim to do is to make these plots just like they was in one
of these old English churchyards, peaceful and quiet like they've
been there centuries." Mr. White . . .' 'I'm sorry I shan't be here
long.' 'Well, I'm sure sorry to hear that. How long you aiming
to stay? You know how it is . . . One day you're . . .' 'No, I'm
sorry, I'm just off.' 'Well now, isn't that too bad. But I want you
to know it's been a great privilege talking to someone like you
from England. Yes, sir, a real privilege.'

Downtown, the huge bill-boards are flooded with light, and
the neon signs flash in and out, in and out, brilliant and magical
and restless like a fairyland gone crazy . . .

Because the advertising, selling and buying of consumer goods
has become the great American religion, the goods themselves
have to be given magical properties far transcending their purely
utilitarian purposes. American advertisers and salesman do not
deal in products. They deal in symbols. Symbols of love, of
potency, of friendship, of success and status – of all that the lost,
the uncertain, the frightened most want.

Consider, for example, what might seem to be the simple
and uncomplicated business of selling belts – men's trouser
belts.

Here is what happened when a New York manufacturer of
belts and suspenders (which the English in their ignorance call
braces) decided to expand. First – this, of course, is practically
mandatory in all American business enterprise, the day of one
man making decisions has long since gone – a Conference was
called. To this Conference were summoned the top managers of
the firm in question, A. Stein and Co., plus outside designers,
advertising experts, research psychologists and authorities on
consumer motivation. These high-powered people had not, of

course, been called together to consider the making of belts. That is a simple matter. Nor did they concern themselves with the quality of the belts. This, although no doubt good enough, was a side issue. What they were gathered together to deliberate on was the much more important matter of the selling of the belt, how, in other words, a trouser belt should be presented and displayed to the public.

Among the eminent authorities summoned was Mr. Louis Cheskin, Director of the Color Research Institute of Chicago and well known as a national authority on the 'symbol area' of package testing, the 'semantic differential in the measurement of advertising affects' and kindred matters. As a result of his intervention a momentous decision was taken: no less than to offer the Stein belts to the public in future not, as used to be customary, hung on a display rack, but packaged in something which should be known as the Vista Dome.

Although the psychological research and field work that followed on this decision were on a scale to strike awe into the breast of any man who has ever, however fleetingly, allowed himself to contemplate keeping up his sports trousers with an old tie, there was, as in all great human decisions, one supreme moment of truth during the proceedings. It came in the course of Mr. Cheskin's address, when the fundamental principle – not to hang but to package – was first introduced.

Mr. Cheskin's speech to the directors, managers, sales executives, designers and advertising advisors of Messrs. A. Stein and Co. is a classic of American salesmanship, and therefore, to some degree, of the American way of life and it contains much of the essence of the magical religion which now has so large a part of the population of the United States in its grip. Here it is, as reported in *Printers' Ink*, and in Mr. Cheskin's own version of a solemn moment in American merchandising in his most recent book, *Why People Buy*. It would be sacrilegious to alter or omit one word.

'The purely functional or practical purpose of a belt is,' he began, 'to hold up a man's pants. However, if people bought belts only for this purpose a man would buy only two or three belts in a lifetime. Actually a string or rope fulfils the practical need. But the average American man is not nearly as concerned with holding up his pants as he is about showing that he owns a beautiful belt, a rare belt, an unusual belt or a costly belt. Beauty, rarity, unusualness and costliness are status symbols. They are psychological factors. They are implements of his ego. They are vital elements of prestige identification.

'Nor does a woman buy a belt for her husband in order to keep his pants up. Every woman knows that a new belt will not be any more effective in keeping her husband's pants up than the old one. When an American woman buys a belt for her man, she is motivated by psychological factors, not practical or functional. She wants the belt because it has symbolic significance. Unconsciously she chooses the type and quality of belt that represents her image of her man. One woman chooses a soft, chamois belt for her man. Another buys an elastic, slick, cowhide strap. A third prefers a rough-surfaced, hard alligator leather. Each type of belt has its character and personality which the woman unconsciously matches to the personality and character of her husband.

'In our highly industrialized complex society, in an economy of abundance, buying a belt is not a mere routine act, as it is in a craft society of low production and consumption sufficient for survival. In an atomic age, the mere act of buying a belt for your husband (or for yourself) is filled with deep psychological implications.

'Marketing tests and experience have shown that normally a woman will not be attracted by belts hanging from a rack. Hanging belts do not arouse a woman's interest. A hanging belt has no attraction power. It is limp, unstimulating and undesirable. To the normal, healthy, energetic woman a hanging belt is not a symbol of virility or quality. It cannot possibly be associated with her man. It is not an appropriate symbol. It presents a negative image.

'The manufacturer of belts who knows what the public wants and respects people's feelings must therefore put the belts in attractive, psychologically meaningful packages. In an appropriate package a belt takes on a personality that it would not possibly have hanging from a rack. An appropriate package reinforces the character of the belt. It protects the belt. It embellishes it. And it does still more, it gives the belt the psychologically meaningful effect of exclusiveness. The fact that the belt is in a package means that it has not been handled by all sorts of people. The package symbolizes additional value, because normally valuable objects are sold in attractive packages. An appropriate package that is an effective marketing tool is no mere physical container. Such a package is endowed with great psychological significance. It is a positive image.

'A belt that is encased in a psychologically potent package symbolizes quality and therefore it easily becomes associated with deep affection or great love. The belt that is housed and protected in a package that has favorable symbolism and psychologically potent color is found worthy of representing deep feeling and is naturally assigned the role of symbolizing respect, affection and even great love.'

After Mr. Cheskin had finished no doubts remained. The decision was taken. The 'Vista-Dome' Pack was born. And as Mr. Cheskin said it would be, so it was – and no doubt will be in England also before long.

In their deliberations and researches, A. Stein and Co. were, according to *Printers' Ink*, principally concerned to find a way to stimulate 'impulse buying'. This, it should be explained, is the opposite of 'reason buying'. Reason buying, although it still rules in industrial purchases, is now becoming progressively less important in American consumer buying, as it will presumably in English buying also, if American advertising experts have their way. Emotion is taking over.

So much is this so that, according to one authority, Mr. Peter R. Smaltz, Director of Marketing Courses, Gannon College, whose books on salesmanship are widely used in American University and College courses on advertising, the pattern of buying in super-markets has completely altered in the last few years. Ten years ago seven out of ten food articles bought at American super-markets were due to 'reasoned buying, often on the basis of a planned and previously thought-out list'. Today, as a result of 'improved' packaging and display, the exact reverse is the case. 'Seven out of ten food items are impulse-bought.'

According to Mr. Smaltz, a careful and erudite man (if a little weak on syntax sometimes), who publishes as an appendix to his most recent book on Salesmanship the names of no less than 141 books which trainee salesmen should read, the motivating factors which govern consumer buying can be classified in three schools.

The first, or 'Simplification School', 'bases all reasons why people buy on three factors: (a) sex, (b) money, (c) religion.' The second, or 'Psychological School', emphasizes basic motives, such as satisfaction of physical desires and parental love, but adds to them 'many new motivations resulting from modern, complicated American super-market living standards'. These are: (1) self-interested leadership which appeals to pride, vanity, comfort and prestige; (2) imitation, people love to imitate success; (3) possessions; and (4) the desire to construct. Finally, there is the Motivation Research School. This lists eight 'hidden motivators'. These are: (1) emotional security, (2) self-assurance, (3) ego-gratification, (4) creative outlets, (5) love objects, (6) power, (7) sense of belonging and (8) immortality.

It will thus be seen that the American salesman has quite a task. He must create symbols that will stimulate all these motives. Few who have suffered under American advertising will deny him credit for trying hard. Nor can it be doubted that on the whole he has succeeded. Americans borrow more and more to buy more and more because the very act of buying has become for many a therapeutic act. To buy is to gain satisfaction and release from tension. It is to prove oneself to one's fellows. It is to be American. And, like a drug, the need to buy calls for ever bigger doses.

A large dispenser of this drug is now getting ready to stimulate British appetites. In January 1962 Safeway Stores, the second largest and the most thrusting of the great American super-market chains, whose 2,000 super-markets in California and the rest of the States deploy every available resource of presentation of display to ensure that once inside one of its shining temples of commerce you wind up at the pay desk with a full trolley, announced that a British subsidiary with £3,000,000 to spend 'for a start' was getting ready to move in and that agents had already been flown out to hunt for stores. Let Mr. Smaltz enlighten us on the days ahead.

To stimulate the appetite of the American consumer to greater and greater excess is now, he states, the main purpose of most American advertising and salesmanship. 'Trading up,' writes the knowledgeable Mr. Smaltz, 'has become the prize objective of the super-markets or self-service stores today. Larger sizes, more units, better quality – all make their challenge for better selling, better packaging, better advertising . . . First there was the economy size, then family giant size, super economy size, gigantic saving size ... Once a home party was complete with one quart of ice-cream, now if two gallons of ice-cream are not within reach a housewife just isn't modern.'

Two gallons of ice-cream where once there was only a quart. It is not the last word on American civilization. But it sometimes seems to be a good deal of the way there. And it represents a large part of its exportable image.

7

The Making of the Group

SHORTLY after the war I was invited to write an article for
Fortune which roused a certain amount of controversy at the time
and was subsequently reprinted as a chapter in a volume entitled
Modern Political Thought: The Great Issues, edited by Professor
William Ebenstein of Princeton. As a visitor from a country
commonly believed by many Americans at that time to be of a
dull grey colour because of post-war austerities, and also in some
danger of becoming a 'socialist prisonhouse', I was invited to say
how I found things in the United States after a stay of several
months compared with life in Britain and other European
countries I knew.

I felt it best to be honest. I began therefore by telling my
American readers that I was more conscious of strain and anxiety
in American society than in that of any other European country
I had experienced. It seemed to me, I said, impossible to live long
in the United States without becoming aware of the stresses and
conflicts imposed upon men and women by the enormous
insistence upon material success as the primary test of human
value, nor without being conscious of the point of no return to
which this salesman's philosophy was in some danger of bringing
them.

But there was also, I added, something else which was perhaps
even more surprising. This, to quote the article as it appeared in
Fortune, was: 'A sense of being imprisoned, confined within a
pattern that has no mercy upon the non-conformist and dictates

what it is sociably acceptable to eat, to wear, to read, to say, to think, and, above all, to set as one's professional goal to an extent that it is not true of any European country I know.'

I suggested that this moulding of the individual to a conventionally acceptable type was not less significant nor less frightening because it was not due to the dictation of a man or of a group of men, as in totalitarian societies, but to a philosophy which increasingly, so it seemed to me, regarded human beings as exclusively mass producers and mass consumers and withheld social approval from all who did not wholly accept the standards of success that it laid down. This conformist pattern, of which I was much more aware than on previous visits, did not, I said, seem natural for American men and women, which was, no doubt, why neurosis was assuming (if one could judge from newspaper reports, medical warnings and what appeared to be an almost universal preoccupation with digestion) the stature of a national disease. It was, I urged, contrary to what is best in the American tradition of freedom and individuality and also to human nature, which surely, I said, had more exacting goals to seek than a well-appointed penitentiary of economic man at the end of a neon-lit road.

That was written twelve years ago. It seemed to me when I returned to the States in 1961 that it had become even more true with the passage of time.

The observations of the visitor are echoed by the lamentations of the resident. In the last few years a vast library has been created, devoted to the melancholy task of telling Americans where their society has gone sour on them – *The Organisation Man*, *The Waist High Culture*, *The Hidden Persuaders*, *Madison Avenue, U.S.A.*, *The Ugly American*, *The Status Seekers*, *The Lonely Crowd*, *A Nation of Sheep* – the titles run on and on, selling in their hundreds of thousands to those who hope that by reading about their condition they will somehow change it.

Within the ambit of their private lives many Americans – organized, status ridden, sheeplike and secretly persuaded though they may be – still find it possible to live happy, amusing and in some cases even eccentric lives. Civilization, one might say, keeps breaking in. The energy of American society is such that the conformist conscience cannot hope to confine it all. Within this immense mass there is room even for originality to hide.

Nevertheless, the elements that make for regimentation are the dominant ones. It is these that are most exportable and most likely to be exported, for they are the most necessary to the specifically American concept of a high consumption, high credit, advertisement dominated, mass production society which American business seeks to transmit. This is not to say that all these elements in American life are transplantable to England. But they cannot be ignored, nor their results on their own society overlooked, in considering just what the American invasion of Britain could involve.

America once presented to the world the face of rugged individualism. It is this face which many attracted by the American invasion still see. But does it still exist? To the visitor returning after an absence it sometimes seems, on the contrary, that America is now becoming to a degree greater than any other society except the Russian, the prime exemplar of 'the group'. This may well have been always inherent in the American condition and in the immense assimilation of races which makes the American experience so unique. However, for many Americans, the fact is obscured by the myth. Among the most cliché-ridden people on earth, they continue to affirm their pioneering allegiance to individuality even as the circumstance of their lives subverts with greater force each day the truth of what they say: perhaps the mould in which modern American organization compresses the human spirit is so contrary to the natural grain of personality that only those who believe the exact opposite to be happening to them could submit to it.

To understand the consequences of American invasion one must first disentangle the American reality from the American myth.

In most countries the major drives to conformity express themselves in political acts. To some degree this is true even in the United States. The influence of both Federal and State governments has grown, is growing and will manifestly continue to grow. That of particular political instruments, like the Senate Committee on Un-American Activities in McCarthy's day and since, reaches down into the private lives of private citizens to an extent no other State but a Communist one would permit.

However, political action, whether of the administrative or inquisitorial kind, is commonly conducted in such an atmosphere of private and public bargaining between the various agencies of government, and between all of them and innumerable pressure groups, that credence is given to the popular belief that a rugged individualism is still paramount in their national affairs. Moreover, the system of checks and balance in the American constitution and the nature of the American parties, so much more concerned with winning electoral power than organizing it politically when it is won, both help to confirm the impression that political power is much less monolithic than where more disciplined parties exist.

Despite the immense growth in the power of central Government over the years there is something in this. Much of American politics is still conducted as a free-for-all. Not all the fights are fixed. It is still harder for an American Government to get what it wants done than it is for a British one. Unless, of course, National Security comes in. Then the sky is the limit and an American Government can mount the most ill-conceived of operations without challenge from public opinion, Press, or political opposition until it is over. (A comparison of the docility of the American Press during the Cuban affair compared with the attitude of an important part of the British Press at the time of Suez is revealing.) But in education, social welfare, economic policy and most other domestic issues the American dream still requires that anarchy shall seem to have its way.

The interests which actually shape American life are much helped by this. The untidiness and irresponsibility of much American politics, while alarming to foreign observers concerned with the efficiency of the democratic process, serves to distract the attention of Americans themselves from what is actually happening to them, perpetuating an image of independence and individuality which not only bears little resemblance to the true state of affairs, but provides a mask behind which conformity can do as it wills.

The American dream has become an instrument for blocking social action by the Government – where it would be public and capable of popular control – in order that it can be handed over to the private decisions of private managements, trade associations and professional bodies who need tell no one what they are up to. The one is anti-democratic because it involves public decision. The other is democratic because it does not.

Freedom, it has often been said, is more than a word. But this is not so for large numbers of modern Americans. For them it is the word that counts. So long as the word is uttered in the right places at the right times in the right tone of voice (even though some of the voices belong to dubious characters using the word for their own dishonourable purposes) all is well. It does not matter that the real pressures in American life increasingly operate to restrict the freedom of ordinary Americans to behave, or act, or think in any way different from others. The word remains.

The process which has made this double standard possible, this march of the American people to conformity with songs of freedom on their lips, begins at school.

American education is admirable in many ways. It is no more free than the rest of American society from class awareness – the sin that must never be mentioned. Yet, despite the pernicious adolescent influence of many of the fraternities and sororities and the agonies imposed on those who do not make the grade, it does not, generally speaking, promote the mushy, patronizing, self-regarding, self-destroying, all-pervading, flim flammery of social caste which the worst of the English public schools still do their best to perpetuate.

In one respect, however, the American High School is like the English Public School. It has extra-pedagogic functions of much greater importance than its academic responsibilities, such as they are.

The Public Schools grew to wealth and influence in the nineteenth century because they possessed, or were believed to possess, a formula capable of turning the sons of businessmen into gentlemen. (With changing times they now have to do the opposite.) From often unpromising material they created peers, bishops, landed gentlemen and a continuous supply of bearers of the white man's burden capable of governing inferior races without emotion or self-doubt and dressing for dinner in the middle of jungles. They have moved on a lot since then but they did the job well when it was what was expected of them.

The first job of the American schools was to make Americans. Like the public schools they too have moved on. But this still remains their primary task.

Americans are by definition equal. Their students must, therefore, be made in this image – or at least treated as if they are. However, it is possible to take some of the pain out of equality by a judicious choice of where to live. Most American children go to the same sort of school. But equality does not have to embrace social promiscuity. All that is needed to avoid it is a good address. In American society the choice of a building lot takes the place of the choice of a Public School in England.

Such short cuts are not available in the field of intellectual training. Here the American dream cannot be handed over to the realtors: educationists have to shoulder it themselves. They are beginning to find the load heavy. 'Can we,' asked one of the most distinguished of them, Dr. John W. Gardner, President of the Carnegie Foundation, in a sub-title to his most recent book – 'Can we be equal and excellent too?'

Of course, the American dream does not require that all men shall actually be equal, or even be treated as if they are. Far from it. But what it does require is that it shall never be admitted that they are not. (In the terminology of American education for example, those incapable of benefiting from ordinary education are not 'educationally sub-normal'. They are 'exceptional'.)

In pursuit of this negative commitment (if it is negative, for after all it can be argued that even the refusal to recognize what exists is in its way a positive act and certainly has positive consequences), American education has done its best to provide millions of Americans with the same tastes and the same social attitudes.

As wave upon wave of immigrants arrived from Southern and

Eastern Europe at the turn of the century to converge upon the cities along with thousands upon thousands of illiterate farm workers drawn there by the promise of higher wages in the new factories and workshops of the industrial era, the rapidly expanded school system found itself called upon to handle a situation such as no educational system in history had had to meet before. Much of the current face of America derives from this unique experience. For what was in the beginning historically necessary has now become economically so. It is part of the just price that has to be paid for the highest material living standards on earth.

To produce future workers able to take their places in the assembly lines of factories in which complicated processes had been broken down into innumerable repetitive tasks capable of being performed quickly and efficiently by those without special skill was comparatively simple. It was no more (or not much more) than the elementary schools of other nations had to do to serve the industrial revolution.

But no other educational system had the double, or rather the treble, task of producing, often from the most intractable raw material, the G.I.s (and most of the officers) of an immense new mass-production force, while at the same time creating out of a bewildering concentration of races, drawn from the most diverse political, social and historical backgrounds and motivated in their migration by the most varied and often mutually antagonistic emotions and ambitions, a quite new human species, the American. And doing so, moreover, while proclaiming with hand raised high, that all were equal, even though they might find it hard to believe so when they looked around them at the different rewards doled out to different people.

This difficult – indeed almost impossible – assignment was carried out with remarkable success. However, in the process the High Schools and State colleges had to throw overboard much of what education had previously been about.

Now they are trying to pick some of it up again. 'Schools Are For Learning,' announced the new Dean of Columbia Teachers College in a 'provocative' message to his colleagues in the autumn of 1960. This revolutionary doctrine, which owed a good deal to the impact on American life of the first Russian sputnik, is now sweeping through American education, leaving a mixture of hope, enthusiasm, distress and frustration in its train.

There were, of course, always a scattered few, even in the American public school system, who believed in learning. And many more in the higher establishments of American education — although fewer in State Colleges and Universities, apart from a few outstanding ones like California, than in private ones. However, for American public education as a whole, the doctrine that 'schools are for learning' is, in hard truth, a new philosophy painfully arrived at. 'But there it is,' as the San Francisco Superintendent of Schools, a great 'life adjuster' in his day, regretfully told his teachers after Sputnik I, 'you've got to re-tool your plant to fit the needs of the time.'

No one can tell what will happen when Americans are educated – any more, of course, than one can what would happen if the English were. As of now, however, the social face America presents for emulation by the world is not the product of education in any sense in which the word is commonly used in an intellectually adult society. It is the end result of the most sustained effort in applied conformism in the history of the world.

When social reformers at the beginning of the century saw in the publicly owned schools the one agency capable of Americanizing the immigrants they set in motion a train of circumstances which was perhaps bound to lead step by step to the all-American consumer of today. For in such a context what was seen as important in education was not that it should provide the tools to enable men and women to think for themselves but the incentive to think and behave like others.

'Life adjustment' courses, 'social adaptation' classes, the requirements of 'community living', these are the educational influences that have most shaped modern America. To the Junior and Senior High Schools have come the bright, the eager, the dull, the ambitious, the active and the indolent of all races and both sexes to be taught that the chief aim of life is to be indistinguishable from other Americans. To be popular and socially acceptable, to learn to belong and be together, to do what others do and be as others are; these have been the tests of achievement and, as we shall see later, very often also, the standards by which suitability for the kind of education that makes for success in later life has been judged.

As often happens, the pragmatism that looked for means to integrate the immigrant found a theoretician at hand to give it a wider and, as it seemed, more eternal sweep, in the philosopher, John Dewey. 'All education,' declared Dewey, 'proceeds by the participation of the individual in the social consciousness of the race . . .' Under this banner American education advanced.

To the outsider, particularly perhaps the European outsider, what is likely to seem most striking about American education, as he eavesdrops on High School life at a Commencement Ceremony or reads the voluminous pages of a High School magazine annotated by a student's notes on who is 'most likely to succeed', is its combination of ruthlessness and sentimentality. It is ruthless in its insistence on the values of the group, sentimental in its anxiety to guard the young from the disappointments of intellectual struggle; some schools put several years of educational time to waste by postponing for all subjects that seem likely to be too hard for some. To Dewey, the prophet, 'the law for presenting and treating material' was 'the law implicit in the child's own nature'. The 'true centre' of education was 'not science, nor literature, nor history, nor geography but the child's own social activities'. It thus became essential that childish nature should not lose the stimulus of success or be affronted by the necessity to do anything intellectually difficult.

I was in New York on one occasion when a High School boy called at his teacher's house after school and shot her through the window with a sawn-off shot-gun. This seemed to me a puzzling way to behave and I asked a boy at the same school what he thought was the reason for it. His answer was eminently reasonable. 'She kept him down a grade,' he said, 'and American boys don't like to fail.'

Nor do they. It has been the business of American schools to establish a framework in which all, even the dullest, can be made to feel that they are succeeding – not, which would be sensible,

by presenting them with tasks within their capacity while others
of greater intellectual capacity tackle work within theirs, but by
relating the pace of learning to the speed of the slowest and by
breaking down, so far as possible, such learning tasks as are
unavoidable into simple components, much as the production
engineer in a mass-production factory does with processes of
manufacture.

The child leaving school after an education inspired by
principles such as these might be thought likely to be singularly
ill-prepared for the complexities of adult life. This is not necessarily so in a conformist society. Or at any rate not on a superficial
social level, whatever may be the case at the deeper levels of
human personality where those neuroses develop to which, to
judge by the part played by the psychiatrist in modern American
life, Americans are more prone than others. It is, indeed, in a
sense the peculiar triumph of the American social system that it
has managed to make the life of the American adult worthy of
his education.

The need for decision, even on the lowest levels of activity
which normally confronts the adult in other societies: What
shall I eat? What shall I buy? What shall I say? has in this been
diminished or removed by establishing for most people a
restricted number of permissible choices. Social life has been, as
it were, programmed in much the same way as a computer is
programmed to ensure the correct responses, or as the latest
gadget of American education, the teaching machine, is programmed to enable a child to learn by flicking a button.

Thus, in all but the most expensive American restaurants (and
the habit is now spreading to British ones) the customer is likely
to find himself with a limited number of standard combinations
to choose from, often to be ordered by number. This makes life
simple for him, simple for the waitress, simple for the cook. To
get something outside the combination – one egg, say, instead of
two or, as my wife once ordered in a Chicago restaurant, one
lamb chop instead of a couple – is, however, almost impossible.
Even to try is to mark oneself as a dangerous deviant determined
to gum up the works. 'And what,' the waitress asked my wife,

'do you think we're going to do with the other chop? It says two chops, doesn't it?' 'Madam,' said a waiter on another occasion, this time in New York, 'what we have is two poached eggs, ham and French fried with salad on the side. You want one poached egg and no French fried you'll have to wait an hour.'

In considering the influence of American education on American life and on the consumers' paradise we are now being invited to join one must also not overlook how much, in that country, education is a woman's business. This is partly because of the predominance of woman teachers. In America, to an even greater extent than in Britain, the financial rewards of teaching are relatively too small to attract the status-hungry male who must demonstrate his manhood in more competitive fields of endeavour. But over and above this the simple biological fact that girls tend to mature two years ahead of boys gives an altogether disproportionate influence to girls in a co-educational school society, based, as the American is, on 'social adaptation' and group popularity.

Dr. Margaret Mead has lately expressed the opinion that the consequences of this are now to be seen in the unwillingness of American young men to set their sights on jobs that need working and studying for, or to take risks in order to do something worthwhile. She considers that American young men are made into domestic pussy cats too young. Patted – and petted – into shape in their most formative years by girls of the same chronological age who are two years older in physical and mental maturity, pressed on by mothers who are terrified lest they should be thought not normal if they do not date while still at High School, imprisoned by student conventions (laid down by girls) that assume that if you date a girl twice you are serious, and helped into early marriage by the belief that employers look with most approval on those who early demonstrate their intention to settle down and have a nice American family, they find themselves pinned fast to domesticity before life has well begun, their incomes pledged years ahead to meet the payments on the house, the furniture, the dishwasher and the car.

The American male, says Dr. Mead, is left without a corner in his suburban home to call his own. With modern American domestic architecture what it is he cannot even find anywhere to hide anything from his wife. He is no longer an independent human being. He is a provider whose eyes must not turn upwards to the stars but fix on a safe job in a big corporation with a pension at the end.

'What have we to do then – marry old men?' asked an indignant High School miss at one of Dr. Mead's lectures to which I went. 'Yes,' said Dr. Mead, 'old men of twenty-four.' It seemed to be considered an unhelpful reply by most of the youthful members of her audience.

It would be improper for an outsider to intervene in Dr. Mead's sorrowful argument with her fellow countrymen. But certainly one consequence of American education and of the immense deference paid to youth in American society – the young must not be thwarted by the old, they must have a better time than their parents, they must have automobiles of their own when they are sixteen, they must not be made to do what they do not want to do – is that Americans are marrying younger and having children earlier. One's first impression of a college campus these days is likely to be the number of young couples wheeling baby carriages on it.

Not all the marriages stick of course. More and more Americans are getting married and are marrying earlier. But the number of those who get divorced is increasing even faster. It has gone up by 28 per cent in the last ten years. This is a reflection of that American conviction – written so deeply for so long into the school system – that life owes Americans an easy ride. If a lesson is too difficult you alter or postpone it, if a job is unpleasant you leave it, if a wife or a husband is hard to get along with you try another one. There is always – there must be for that is what it means to be American – a new life the other side of the range.

Of course there are many American marriages that last. The conception of American society as one long round of matrimonial musical chairs with everyone popping in and out of everyone else's bed while the delinquent children live it up on the back porch or race about the country in beaten-up sports cars, working out their hatred of the adult world with violence, casual fornication and marijuana, presumably touches reality here and there. How else would all those popular novelists get all that material for all those long novels? But it is constantly contradicted by the number of pleasant people living pleasant lives in the bosom of their pleasant families with the same wives and husbands as they have always had and sons and daughters neither less nor more affectionate than elsewhere. Nevertheless, in this society of waning cultures the tides of American life are running against them.

Like all nations, the United States sees itself in the image of its past. This past is so recent that it looms larger in what Americans say and think about themselves than in most cultures. Nor have all the pioneering qualities been lost. The American energy, the immense American competence in material things, the power and sweep of American engineering, of American road-building and American construction, their mastery of steel and concrete and their vigour in shaping the physical elements of their inheritance to their will, all these are still real and potent in the American scene.

But the American character, founded on the overcoming of physical difficulties and dangers, and still at its most admirable and creative when presented with such tasks, is more susceptible than most to the attrition of success. They are a people easily softened by ease. The pioneering virtues of independence and individuality that still set much of America's image for the world have become a self-deceiving legend. They bear less and less resemblance to what Americans actually are. The Daguerreotype has become a glossy print.

8

The Label on the Pack

'DON'T sell the steak, sell the sizzle,' advised one of the most successful of the founding fathers of modern American advertising – he subsequently started a college of sizzlemanship and wrote no less than fifteen books on the subject. Millions of Americans have been buying the sizzle ever since.

As the itinerant visitor reads through one of those American restaurant menus in which adjective is piled on adjective in a wild frenetic poetry that bears no resemblance whatever to the actual food put before him, with its flavour of superior deep-frozen cardboard (most British hotel food, on the other hand, tastes like soggy blotting-paper and scarcely pretends to be anything else), or wanders, dazed by prolixity, through one of those enormous super-markets we are so sure to enjoy for our very own, with corridor upon corridor of canned seafood and wrapped bread in which the picture of sliced bacon on the pack bears no relation to the bacon inside, and cans of olives come medium, large, Jumbo, Giant, Colossal, Extra-Colossal, Super-Extra-Colossal and Supreme-Extra-Colossal, he is likely to conclude that most Americans actually prefer the sizzle to the steak.

Nor is it only when thus caught in the middle of the long, gruelling, rumbustious, and, by most civilized standards, basically purposeless, although presumably enjoyable, battle between American salesmanship and its willing victims that the visitor is tempted to think this – although if enjoyable why do so many of those pushing their wire trolleys up and down the long aisles, a miniature calculating machine for sound budgeting on one handle, seem caught in so hypnotic a daze? A similar dichotomy between words and reality exists in most other areas of American life. In fact, probably the best service American education could now do Americans would be to organize courses in semantics to enable them to relate what they do to what they say.

America is drunk with words. As one moves across the country the glossy packs in the super-markets take on a sad symbolic significance. One suddenly realizes that the package has acquired so great a reality of its own that hardly anyone any longer knows, and perhaps hardly cares, what is inside it. The label is printed, the appropriately emotional colour chosen, the cellophane wrapper completed. What the package says becomes itself the actuality, in the way that children, when very young, believe that to put a thought or a fear or a longing into words it to make it come true; that to say is to do.

This is why Russia's success in space came as such a peculiarly horrid shock to American public opinion. Fed on the legend that what America does is, by a law of nature, bigger and better than that done by anyone else (many G.I.s transported on the *Queen Elizabeth* and the *Queen Mary* during the war stoutly refused to believe that these ships, 'the biggest in the world', had not been built in America), the first sputnik created extraordinary dismay and bewilderment.

One consequence was a mass revulsion on the part of automobile buyers against the tail fins, chrome and three-tone body finishes they had previously been clamouring for. Before Sputnik I more than 95 per cent of car owners in a General Motors' survey asked for chrome, after it the number dropped to less than half. Shocked and numbed by the news that they were running second to Russia in the space race, millions of Americans turned to the central symbol of their way of life, and asked for a different packaging.

But the demoralization went much deeper than this and was one of the reasons why, on a later occasion, it was impossible for most Americans to share in that sense of a great moment in human history which made the British people turn out in their thousands to cheer Gagarin when he came to London. ('You ought to be grateful they didn't send the dog,' Mr. Macmillan is reported, wrongly I am sure, to have cabled to Mr. Kennedy when the President protested that surely London's reception was a little excessive.) For their own friends to applaud a Russian for doing something an American had not – this seemed the most hateful of treacheries.

One became conscious as one talked to many Americans at the time that the firm earth had shaken under their feet. Both the labels they had been given to live by had been proved wrong: the American label on America which told them that no country in the world could hope to emulate their free-enterprise system in technical knowledge and know-how; the American label on Russia which assured them that no Communist could ever achieve the technological expertize of a free American – just as, many years before, Mr. Henry Ford's Production Manager, Charles M. Sorenson, had come back from Moscow with the good news that 'anything that means mass production has the Communists licked'.

Although the shock of Russia's achievements in space shook popular morale to an extent that seems altogether excessive in the light of America's own resources of scientific knowledge and power, it would be too much to hope that it has permanently altered the American belief in labels. Indeed, observing some aspects of American foreign policy, one sometimes has the feeling that they would rather lose a battle than a label – better, for example, to strain the United Nations to breaking point than take a second look at Formosa or any other of the seedy 'bastions of freedom' with which American policy litters the Far East and paves the way to Communism; or drive Cuba wholly and finally into Russia's arms (if they have not already done so) than change the tag.

However, it is no part of the purpose of this particular volume to trace the cost in Asia, South America and Africa of the American determination to believe the label on the packet, especially when it is an American label. Mr. Lederer and Mr. Burdick have already gone a good way to doing so in *The Ugly American* – 'If this were not a free country,' said the *New York Herald Tribune*, 'this book would be banned,' making one wonder since when a great American newspaper has felt that freedom to publish called for self-congratulation.

What I am concerned with here, are the more subtle deceptions which combine to make the real face of America so different from what those in Britain who welcome Americanization imagine it to be – or what most Americans think it is.

The label tells Americans and the world that theirs is the most classless of all societies – the one with the greatest freedom of opportunity for talent.

It is this quality which naturally enough makes the idea of America attractive to the people of other countries – and particularly to the young and under-privileged. Once it was true enough and it was part of the American glory that it was. But to a foreign observer in love with the America he first knew it seems to be becoming less true with almost every year that passes.

So far from being a tough, individualistic people glorying in the competitive fight, the American people are now building for themselves a society increasingly stratified in its social structure. They have stopped being pioneers and became bureaucrats. Instead of dreaming of fighting their way from the wrong side of the tracks to wealth and power, they grab a safe job with a pension the first chance they get.

Much of this change is, of course, unavoidable and has been developing over a long time: great industrial societies cannot be left to the mercy of tycoons and still less to that of failed tycoons – which even at the height of tycoonery was, in the nature of things, what most of the tycoon-minded were compelled to be. But in the process of change something formerly very precious to the American dream is now being lost – the way to the top: the sense (however remote from what actually happened to most) that America was a land of limitless opportunity and that there was no reason why the man on the machine floor today should not be the company president tomorrow.

His chance of doing so now is much less than it was. Despite British snobbery and taste for social class, it is, in fact, probably a good deal smaller than in Britain or several other European countries. There is a lot in Mr. Vance Packard's remark in *The Status Seekers*: 'Although Americans still tend to think of equality as being peculiarly American, and of class barriers as being peculiarly foreign, the evidence indicates that several European nations such as Holland, England and Denmark, have gone farther than America in developing an open class system where the poor but talented young can rise on their merits.'

Materially, the American industrial worker is still the best off in the world. Despite war and post-war improvements in wages and living conditions the average British worker still lags a good way behind him. As an example, longshoremen in San Francisco can expect to earn an average of $6,500 a year (roughly just over £44 a week) without overtime and with guaranteed employment, and when I attended one of their union Locals I was told of several who with overtime averaged annual earnings of between $8,000 and $10,000. Nor would one expect to find at a British dockside the vast San Francisco parking lot reserved for longshoremen.

The difference between the living standards of the middle and professional classes in the two countries is nothing like so great. I know several young British people with temporary appointments in the States who were offered permanent ones. After taking into account not only the ordinary cost of living but such things as the potentially crippling cost of medical attention in America in the event of serious illness, the cost of insurance, the substantial savings they would have to put by for the higher education of their children as compared with the position in Britain with its free Grammar School and University education including maintenance where needed, and the relative cheapness of such cultural amenities – or necessities – as theatres, music, books, and even newspapers in England, they decided that there was not enough in it to make much difference economically, or to compensate for what seemed to them the greater variety and depth of English life.

But although differences at the middle-class level are marginal they are not so at the working-class level. The American industrial worker not only earns a good deal more than his British or European counterpart, he earns a good deal more, even when the rise in cost of living is taken into account, than he did ten years ago. He pretty certainly lives in a better house than he did then and unless he is one of the 5,000,000 unemployed his union has probably won him more security in his job.

But if his material position has risen spectacularly in the last ten or twenty years, his relative social position has fallen and his social mobility declined. He has a bigger car. (To casual observers from older communities where possession of a car still has more social significance than in the United States this often suggests a higher social rating than is in fact the case.) But however ambitious and hardworking he may be his chances of moving into the next social group up are becoming steadily smaller. So are his prospects of getting a foot on to even the lower rungs of the management ladder.

This is partly due to the sheer fact of bigness. In all bureaucracies the division between officers and other ranks tends to become more formalized than in smaller, more fluid groupings. And American industry is being bureaucratized on an enormous scale. As the *Wall Street Journal* reported at the conclusion of one of its management surveys, 'The corporate caste system is being formalized and rigidified in more and more American companies.'

Even nine years ago, a *Fortune* survey of the leading executives of the three hundred largest industrial, railroad and public utility concerns in the United States showed that the chances of anyone who lacked a good middle- or upper-class background, including at least four years at a university, reaching the top levels of corporation management had already become very small and was getting smaller. Only 8 per cent of the leading executives of these industrial groups had any working-class background. Among those under fifty the proportion had fallen to less than $2\frac{1}{2}$ per cent. Since then lack of a middle-class background and a college education has become even more of a bar to an executive job and the social position that goes with it.

This is far less so in Britain. According to an Acton Trust

survey, less than a fifth of British managers under the age of fifty are drawn from the kind of family and university background that is now increasingly mandatory in American industry. And although the proportion of university graduates under the age of thirty-five has risen to about one in three and is still rising, many more graduates now come from lower middle- or working-class backgrounds.

In a society where the ideal is 'a college education for every kid' it may not seem much of a social bar to demand a university degree from every would-be administration man. But whether the idea that they should is sensible or not, the majority of American kids do not, in fact, go to college, despite the popular myth to the contrary in Britain as well as America.

About half those who go to High School do not even try to, and of those who do only three-fifths actually make it. About seventy per cent of the total High School population is as a result now ruled out from entering for the executive stakes before the race even begins. Many more fail to qualify, for although in nearly half the States the State University is required to take all applicants with a High School diploma, a great many do not stay the course. At the University at Madison, Wisconsin, for instance, I was told that it was usual for at least 40 per cent to drop out, or be turned out, by the end of the first year.

Nor are all even of the State universities prepared to take all who graduate at High School. The biggest, the University of California, takes only the top $12\frac{1}{2}$ per cent of High School graduates, which means out of the school population as a whole approximately the same proportion as qualify for university entrance in Britain – the rest of those who want higher education have to make do with lower-level State Colleges and Junior State Colleges.

Academically this is sensible from the point of view of university standards. But in an increasingly bureaucratized society in which entry into management, accountancy, law and architecture or even such semi-professions as journalism is more and more barred to those who do not possess a university qualification, it means that professional and social advancement is made steadily more difficult for the non-university majority – far more so than in Britain.

So, far from being an open society with plentiful opportunities for talent from whichever side of the tracks it comes, America is in danger of becoming an extremely rigid one.

Nor, despite American shudders at the British eleven-plus examination as 'undemocratic', is this danger lessened by the methods American education itself employs for selecting potential university students.

Those who are to be permitted to make a bid for the university career that increasingly offers them their only chance of a job with status and prospects are picked in the Junior High. These are not, as you might think in view of the importance of their function, institutions specially qualified for the task. On the contrary in many areas they tend to be, in the words of one recent writer on American education (Mr. Martin Mayer in his massive volume, *The Schools*), 'the dumping ground of the school system'. So much is this the case, in fact, that in New York, it has been found hard to persuade qualified teachers to serve in them. As a result, half the teachers in New York Junior High Schools do not even hold a teachers' certificate*. Moreover, the quality of Junior High Schools — as also of Senior High Schools— varies enormously throughout the country, not only from State to State but from school district to school district within each State. And since the schools are locally financed and locally managed, the level of education and the facilities for learning available to children in the suburbs and middle-class areas are normally much superior to those available to children from poor or even ordinary working-class areas. Discrimination begins with where you live.

At the Junior High, America's future élite is not picked on an intelligence or academic basis. That would be 'undemocratic'. Although their academic, and professional future depends on its selection processes students are not, in fact, expected to do much academic work in the Junior High. This is the period of 'social adjustment'. The choice of those who are to be groomed for preferment is therefore largely determined by 'orientation' and

* Do not teach subjects for which they have been licensed would be a more accurate statement.—Ed.

'guidance' talks, aptitude tests, class discussions on 'the world at work', and advice by the 'guidance counsellor' on how to set 'realistic goals' for yourself.

At the end of these the child is guided to 'elect' which of several programmes he will take in the ninth grade, and so on through his life at Senior High. He can 'elect' for the 'vocational programme', the 'general or business programme', neither of which are concerned with higher education in the usual sense, or the 'academic programme', which is.

It is a momentous decision, for on this choice depends in large measure not only the course of a boy's or girl's school career but also their adult career. The vocational programme means education suitable for a manual worker, the general or business programme education for an office job at the clerk or typist level. Only the 'academic' programme makes available the kind of education that can lead to college entrance – not of course that it will necessarily do so; on average about four out of ten of those 'electing' to take it fail to make the grade.

Once a boy or girl has 'elected' for a programme, that is it: subsequent transfer from 'vocational' to 'business' or from 'business' to 'academic' is, for all practical purposes, out. It is, in most cases, far more difficult to make such a transfer than it is, for instance, to move from one stream to another in a comprehensive school or from a secondary modern to a grammar school in Britain when a second look at a boy or girl in their teens suggests that as desirable, or than it is for a French boy or girl to move over from an unacademic to an academic course in school.

In principle – and principle is in all such matters very important to the American dream; almost more important than practice – the purpose of this 'elective' system is to guide American children in the way most likely to make them happy and 'socially adjusted', and no doubt the school guidance counsellors bend their energies to this end as honestly as they can.

The decisions reached are, however, by the nature of the means used, largely subjective and in many instances more weight is given to social and family backgrounds than to intellectual ability. Indeed, in his exhaustive study of youth in a

typical Middle Western community (*Elmtown Youth*), Professor
A. B. Hollingshead, at that time at the University of Chicago,
now at Yale, found that it was taken for granted by most High
School children that the High School grades were directly related
to their parents' social positions, and his own investigations
indicated that there was a good deal of truth in this. The teacher
who had held her post longest at the High School and was most
highly regarded by the school managers (drawn almost exclusively
from middle- or upper-middle-class groups) was disliked and
distrusted by the majority of children and parents in the three
lower social groups. Those in the two top social groups praised
her because, as one of them said: 'She knows every child's background and treats it accordingly.'

Of course the boy from a working-class family may be guided
to 'elect' for an academic programme. Unless he is very outstanding he is, however, in many cases much less likely to be so
than a boy from a middle-class background. (Just as in one large
Junior High I know in a town where almost a third of the
population is negro it just so happens that very few negro
children are ever guided to elect for an academic programme.
Most go to the vocational programme. 'After all,' I was told,
'it is best to think of their happiness and not to try to tear them
away from their home background.' The State University, open
to children from this High School, is in no sense segregationist.
It is willing to welcome any negroes who arrive with the right
grades. Fortunately or unfortunately it so happens that not
many do – nor very many, for that matter, from white working-
class backgrounds either.) Social adjustment is a worthy phrase.
What it often means in practice is doing what the School Counsellor at the Junior High thinks most suited to your social
background.

Even those from working-class backgrounds who are allowed
to take the academic programme and who ultimately reach college
do not always find it easy to stay there. Tuition will probably
be free – although even in the State universities it is not universally so. But nothing else is. Thus in the University of California,
the largest in the United States, there is no charge for tuition to

State residents but the student must expect to meet annual bills of something over $1,000 to cover other expenses. That is if he is careful. If he is 'liberal', the official literature explains, it will be nearer $1,300 (or about £460) a year – almost the same in cash terms as annual fees to Harrow or Winchester.

The vast majority of students must find this money from their own or their parents' pockets. There are some grants but not many. Compared with the British system under which students of moderate means accepted by a university become eligible for Local Authority grants not only for tuition fees and books but living expenses, this means a level of outlay that is bound to press heavily on, even if it is not beyond the means of, many working-class families, even on American wages.

The American answer is that to work one's way through college is part of the American way of life. No doubt in the past it was and it would be foolish to deny its social value. University students can learn a good deal as soda jerks or car-park attendants.

But as the curriculum of universities becomes more academic and more specialized under the pressure of the 'desire for excellence', and the pass level for degrees is raised, it is getting harder and harder to earn the money to get through college and retain the time and energy to pass grades at the requisite levels. This is one of the reasons for the high wastage from many State Universities in the first two years.

Regular daily work to earn enough money to cover all one's university expenses at a fairly high level is a very different matter from a job in the vacation to help supplement a grant, or a middle-class income, which is now almost as common among British and Continental students as among American. However, when one suggests that the richest country in the world with a need for all the talent it can find might think so too, many Americans get very indignant indeed.

There is, of course, still a good deal of social bias in British education as well as American. The pulling power of a public school tie is less than it was, but it is still there. And within the State system the eleven-plus examination discriminates fairly sharply, and at an even earlier age than the American system does, between potential officer material and other ranks, between those who will go to the Grammar School and those who will go to a Secondary Modern. This discrimination is, however, less final in the British than American society. A significant number of Secondary Modern boys and girls who have originally failed their eleven-plus catch up and either transfer to a Grammar School or take their Certificate of General Education at the Secondary Modern at a level sufficient to enable them to go on to a University, and in some cases to win open State Scholarships over the heads of Grammar School contenders. Within a comprehensive school – the nearest equivalent to an American High School – the transfer from one stream to another is even easier.

There is a good deal to say against the eleven-plus. But at least its selectiveness is not class directed. It discriminates, or tries to, on the basis of academic ability, not social status, and it does so by objective measurements, not the subjective judgements of teachers and school counsellors with an eye on class backgrounds.

This is not, of course, to say that the eleven-plus is the most desirable way of determining the best education for children of differing interests and aptitudes, or that their separation in such sharply divided school groups is not open to a good deal of criticism. Nor is to pretend that the scales in British education are not still weighted in innumerable tangible and intangible ways in favour of those who start life with social advantages.

But although the redbrick revolution has taken long a-hatching, and although it has not gone as far as one might wish, it is a genuine revolution and it is here. The chances of a working-class boy in America ending up with a Plymouth sedan and a home with a deep freeze are pretty high. But his chances of moving across the barriers of class into the executive ranks are not only a good deal lower than they used to be, they are now probably much smaller than those of the boy from a similar background in Britain.

Nor, although the gap between the American dream and the American reality is widening, was social mobility between classes ever as large as the myth suggested. It only seemed so because of the mass of poverty-stricken immigrants who were so low that there was no place for them to go but up, unless, indeed, as many did, they rotted to death in what are still, even now, among the worst city slums in the world.

Some tried to make their way up the fast way and became bootleggers and gangsters – occupations almost exclusively staffed by second generation Southern European immigrants – or, if they were Irish, crooked politicians. But like their counterparts in all industrial communities the great majority of those drawn into the vastly expanding industrial machine, whether from the ranks of farm workers or the immigrants, have always moved upwards not as individuals but as a group, having to fight even harder than most in the early days to organize themselves and get a fair share of the product of their labour.

Nor was the social mobility open to the ruthless, the enter- prising or the talented in nineteenth-century Britain relatively much smaller than in America during the same period. The main difference was that those moving up in Britain found an existing aristocracy at the top that they had to penetrate – although one very susceptible to penetration if there was enough money about. In the United States they had to make an aristocracy of money for themselves. But there is, to take an obvious example, very little difference sociologically speaking between the family history of Mr. Macmillan and President Kennedy. Mr. Kennedy's grand- father may possibly have done better in Boston than he would have done in Liverpool – though many men of his kind did well enough for themselves and their heirs there as anyone can see from even a casual glance at the peerage. It is unlikely that if Mr. Macmillan's crofter grandfather had set up shop in New York instead of London he would have done any better by his grandson than he did.

Nevertheless, there was in the past enough truth in the Ameri- can belief in the limitless opportunities of their society to give a genuine substance to the American dream. The great majority, it is true, neither climbed out of their social group nor particu- larly wanted to. But the belief that they could, or that their sons could even if they did not, combined with the sense of space that was always there to beckon the boldest, did give American society a genuine quality of hope and excitement.

It is both sad and odd, and also very relevant to a current judgement of American society and the welcome that should be given to the American invasion, that this dream of an open society should be fading in the land of its birth just when others are taking it over and giving it a larger connotation.

Not only is the organization of the big corporation becoming increasingly stratified but there is a declining place in American society for that great figure in its earlier tradition, the small man building up his own business by energy, flair and hard work. If you have a drug store or a food store, or a liquor store, or a clothes pressers you may, by staying open until nine or ten at night and on Sundays (and it is still true that no one will stop you doing this as they would in Britain), manage to take some trade away from the big chains and super-markets and stay alive and be your own boss. But it gets harder each year. The small firm is giving way to the big corporation, the private shop to the chain store, even that last relic of individualism in most countries, agriculture, is now more controlled, subsidized and planned for than the agriculture of almost any other country in the world.

America has become a nation of employees. Less than 13 per cent of the working population are now on their own: before the war it was 20 per cent. Moreover, not only are more than 87 per cent of all working Americans on somebody else's payroll, most of them are on the payrolls of a few big organizations. In industry 2 per cent of the firms – the giants – employ more than all of the rest put together.

This, it would appear, is how most Americans want it. According to several recent college surveys, less than 5 per cent of students who go into business have any vision of a future in which they will run things for themselves – or any desire for it. Few want to go into a small or middle-sized firm if they can help it. They prefer to be cogs in large machines. The same is becoming equally true in the professions. The law student or the architect rarely now envisages a day when he will hang up his own shingle on his own office door. He wants a job in a big professional firm.

America is less snobbish than England, but it is becoming more stratified and more class directed. And as the safe jobs in the big organizations cast their shadows farther and farther across the land the influence of class grows steadily stronger.

America may have many things to export, but a working model of a classless society is no longer one of them, nor even one likely to hold out more opportunity to the young and unprivileged than our own. Perhaps in the future the American dream will return. One hopes so, for it was a great dream and the American energy is such that no one in his senses would discount the possibility of its revival as the America people realize what is being lost in their society. But as of now what is most likely to strike the saddened observer is not the freedom and equality of American society but its increasing rigidity.

9

Life by the Layer

ONE evening, walking through the streets of Berkeley, California, I came across a group of people standing on the side walk at an almost deserted intersection. I was just preparing to step into the street when I became aware from the glances I received that public opinion was against me. And so, more readily intimidated in such matters than in my own country, I waited until the walk sign authorized us all to go.

It is absurd, no doubt to see much significance in this. In a country so covered with automobiles as America is it is obviously wise that pedestrians should be trained to obey traffic instructions. Not to cross the road until the indicator says go is sense.

All the same, the way in which this group waited on the side walk of an empty street until authority in the form of a mechanical sign told them they could move sent a small ripple of cold down my spine. It seemed to me an indication of a people in some danger of abdicating personal judgement altogether to authority.

Those of my American friends who have driven in London tell me they consider this very dangerous. One eminent lawyer, indeed, graphically described to me how he had stepped into a rented car outside Brown's Hotel to drive his family into the country and ten minutes later had turned it in, a nervous wreck, with his wife and children weeping in the back and calling on him to stop before he killed either them or someone else.

I do not find it so. I find on the contrary that the knowledge that almost anyone may do whatever comes into his mind at any time and is as likely as not to step into the road at the very moment the signal turns green for traffic makes for a lively and active mind and a readiness for emergencies which is good both for one's driving skill and one's character. And I find the un-willingness as yet of most English people to let the existence of wheeled traffic altogether dominate their lives or inhibit the expression of their individualities encouraging and endearing.

Automobiles are so much a primary symbol of the American religion, having a special, an almost God-like, place in American society that the relationship of the American to his car illustrates in a particularly vivid way a regimentation and authoritarianism that is in fact beginning to spread much wider. Before the needs of the automobile, or its high priests in the Highways Department, freedom must hide its head.

I remember very vividly an evening my wife and I spent at the home of a charming lady of close on eighty who was the aunt of a close friend of ours. Her house was situated in a kind of dell. Flowers and lawns and trees of an infinite variety surrounded it and the house itself, with its large living-room and splendid views, its low bookshelves and grace and comfort, spoke of civilization and the pleasures of the heart and mind. After dinner, all of us, our hostess herself, an old, eminent and very lovable philosopher and his brilliant and vivacious wife, a younger Professor of English Literature with a wife no less intelligent and charming, a young doctor with a political conscience, and the granddaughter of our hostess who was shortly going on her first trip to Europe, sat and talked and then in that delightful American way read poetry to each other.

When the time came regretfully to leave, my wife and I, after thanking our hostess most warmly, said to her, 'You must love this house and garden in which you have lived so long and which you have made so charming.' 'I love it especially now,' she said, 'because in a month's time the Highways Department are moving in with bulldozers to knock it down and fill up the hollow and make a freeway.'

She was far from being alone in this. When we first arrived in

California, the Chairman of the University Department to which
I was attached, and his wife, who were to become two of the
dearest friends we have known in our lives, were in some disarray
because the house in which they lived was about to be flattened
to the ground for the same reason. Later we met a neighbour of
theirs to whom this had happened twice in succession. We heard
of many others.

Indeed we often found subsequently that many of those most
urgent in their assurances that Americans would never submit
to the kind of Governmental controls and planning under which
they conceived our lives in England to be spent, took it as a
matter of course that if the Highways Department decided to
knock down the house in which you had lived for years in order
to cut a new road or build a flyover where none, to the ordinary
eye, was needed, or take out a small and inoffensive kink in an
old road in order that the stream of automobiles should not have
to slow down even for a few seconds, then there was nothing
you either could, or should, want to do about it. The Highways
Department slapped down an order, told you the usually quite
inadequate price it proposed to pay in compensation*, forbade
you to remove anything from either house or garden since you
were being paid, however poorly, for the place as it stood so
that it could cease to do so with the minimum of delay – and
that was that.

Not only the present but all the possible future needs of the
automobile-god must be served. I once heard Senator Barry
Goldwater of Arizona describe in graphic detail the construction
at great cost of immense cloverleaf flyovers in the middle of a
vast, empty desert – presumably to show that Arizona was a
modern state.

Like Romans manqué, the Highways Departments advance in
a straight line whatever treasure of man or nature may stand in
their path. They express in a particularly dogmatic way the
American need to dominate rather than come to terms with the
land in which they live. Outside the Southern States and New
England few American townships have any relationship to their
situation. They do not seek to merge with, and so enrich, the

* From this point on the author appears to have exaggerated.—Ed.

countryside of which they are a part as many small English and
French, Spanish and Italian towns do.

When one flies across America by night this need of Americans
to dominate rather than assimilate the countryside in which they
live strikes one with particular force. Each garish explosion of
neon lights below seems, from the calm above, like a fist shaken
in the face of Heaven – a gesture of defiance against darkness
and the rhythm of life and the immensity of mountain and plain
and desert, and the long, deep-rooted character of the land. They
seem, these frenzied splurges below, to be the creation of men
singing to keep their courage up.

It is peculiarly the American's relationship to the automobile
that also determines the pattern of his suburban life and enables
him to escape from it and take a trip to Arizona or New Mexico
or some place else where you can get away from it all. (Not, of
course, that this is as easy as it was before air-conditioning took
over: 'I awake in my air-conditioned home in the morning, I
take a dip in my swimming-pool. I dress and get into my air-
conditioned automobile and drive to the air-conditioned garage
in the basement of my air-conditioned office block. I work in an
air-conditioned office, eat in an air-conditioned restaurant and
maybe go on to an air-conditioned theatre in the evening,'
explained one denizen of what used to be known as the Arizona
bad lands to a *Saturday Evening Post* reporter.)

These magnificent roads and the no less magnificent automobiles whose purpose they have been built to serve have produced a physical mobility greater than any country has ever
known before. You can drive five hundred miles or more without
getting tired and find at the end of the day a motel exactly as
comfortable and as well fitted as the one you checked out of in
the morning, and in all important respects identical. Even when
one breaks away from the high roads and drives, as we did, with
two cheerful and civilized friends through the wine country of
Northern California with its Italian communities whose lives
still follow patterns only a little different from those of their
Mediterranean brothers (such meals one may eat there) and on to
the wild magnificence of the coast, to eat and doze and talk in

the sunshine beside the Pacific, time's winged automobile is always at one's heels. The mechanical diggers and the bulldozers have already moved in to widen the roads and make new ones. The realtor's signs announcing new sub-divisions and building lots flower in the fields although the crop is still to be harvested.

But although the automobile has made possible what is in many ways an enormously exciting and stimulating physical mobility, it has also become one of the prime servants of the new social immobility of American life as expressed in the one-layer towns and suburbs that are among the newest manifestations of the growing gap between the American reality and the American image.

One of the great attractions to the visitor to the United States is the immense variety of the people who make up the American nation and the easy surface democracy that links them all. Nor is this surface democracy unimportant. The surface of life has its value as well as the depths. The lack of patronage or servility, the ease of acquaintanceship, the absence of the pathetic snobbisms with which the suburban English guard their little lives, the general courtesy and informality of American manners, all these are not only valuable in themselves but true to the American character.

It is true that one cannot always be certain of the informality. There are times and places where a kind of parvenu formality sometimes takes over, sometimes rather touchingly so, as when I unwittingly greatly upset the head waiter of one of those open-air restaurants at the Rockefeller Plaza in New York at which one may eat pleasantly, if not particularly well, under a striped umbrella, by taking off my jacket on one of the hottest days of the year, as I would in any similar, although superior, open-air restaurant in Paris or Rome or Venice. He seemed, poor man, to imagine that it was lowering the tone of the place. However, this may possibly have been because the restaurant was called, for some strange reason, the English Grill: perhaps it was my own persona I was being hoist with.

This surface polish of egalitarianism should not, however, be allowed to deceive: Joe says Hi to many more people and many more people say Hi to Joe than Joe would think of knowing socially.

To an increasing extent the young middle-class couples who live on their credit ratings live in strictly one-layer towns linked to the city or industrial area by fast motorways which have done away with the need to live alongside those of other social classes in the comprehensive townships of the past. The estate developments of which they are a part have been ruthlessly planned by socially wise real estate men to meet the ambitions of specific economic levels – and very often specific ethnic groups. The houses are mass produced to fit sharply defined social expectations. The shopping centre is geared to the exact social and income level – or just a shade above it in order to stimulate buying and create a sense of prestige – of the people who will live in these houses.

Even the churches follow the same pattern: at the top Episcopalian (the preferred religion, according to the evidence of the sociological surveys, of corporation executives by a margin of ten to one), Presbyterian, Congregational and Unitarian just below (perhaps even challenging the Episcopals in some areas in New England), Christian Science for the 'upward mobiles' (the economic status of Christian Science, always fairly high, is moving forward rapidly I was assured by many people and external evidence supported this), the Methodists, the Lutherans, the Baptists following in a descending order, so that you can pretty well judge the social ranking of a suburb by the churches in it – only the Catholics and the Jews cut across the lines.

Within these one-layer towns in which the modern American and his wife can live happily and 'creatively' without ever having to mix with anyone of a different class group, social conventions are as intricate and formalized as those of ancient China although less openly acknowledged. It is necessary to do the same things, play the same games, read the same books, serve the same drinks, think the same thoughts, join the same voluntary organizations, accept the same civic responsibilities, be sociable in the same sort of way. One has joined not a classless society but a one-class society and one must keep within its frontiers.

One's spending must be equally circumspect. One must keep up with the Joneses. But one must not go beyond them – wait to buy some things until the indefinable moment arrives when the sense of the community makes this expenditure proper and acceptable. It is not necessary to have exactly the same as one's neighbours but such differences as there are must be kept within a narrow and well-understood range. Although one must show oneself up and coming one must not put on dog.

The insides of these pleasant houses are all approximately alike, and the cars in the garages are within the same price range. When the times comes, if it does, when promotion makes it possible to spend more, you do not spend it here, you move out to another suburb, to a new one-level town on a higher level, and start all over again. And because this may happen at some time or another – indeed must if you are to make the grade – you are neighbourly but you do not put down roots. When you move do not take your friendships with you. You make new friends.

Within the invisible ring fence of these one-layer communities life is pleasant, sociable, and community minded. You need never be lonely – except perhaps inside yourself. This is the America of stories in English women's magazines and pleasant domestic comedies on the television screen, exciting hopes of emulation in the minds of those for whom it has become as real as their own houses.

When the husband from one of these pleasant suburban homes drives off to work in the morning he moves from one world to another very similar to it – indeed his life at home is likely in many ways to be an extension of his life at work. He lives among young middle-class college graduates. He probably works among them too. It is, of course, mandatory that just as he must be friendly and 'democratic' with the delivery man when he calls at the house, so must he also be with any of the lower grades of workers in his organization he may have to meet. But he and they know very well that he is in a different slot and what that slot is.

Just as it is the group that counts in the suburb, which suspects individualists and expects those who live there to fit in, so it is the group that counts at work, especially if he is, as so many young Americans now strive to be, employed by a big organization. He must set himself all the time to be as like the other members of the group at his level – good fellows all, upstanding young American business men with keen minds and hair on their chests – as he can. He must avoid being different. American industry and business does not want geniuses any more – indeed, many of them go to considerable, and, as it seems, when one first comes across their announcements, surprising, pains to make this clear in their personnel advertisements. They want hard-working young Americans who will fit into the team and do what is expected of them. That is what they want.

American business is increasingly geared to recruiting and cherishing the ordinary, the ordinary that is with the right background and college degree. It is increasingly geared, also, to the belief that this ordinariness can best be found and nurtured and in due course selected for promotion by mechanistic means. What is important is the norm – the man who will play along with the rest, who will be keen, but keen in the right way, who will sink his personality in the group and recognize that it is group decisions that are important.

He is likely therefore, having got the necessary college and social background, to be selected for his first job, and also for his second one if he should ever change his employer (employment mobility is steadily diminishing at the executive grade level: one move is the most that the ambitious man is likely to allow himself and an increasing number stay through all their careers within the secure walls of the same organization), not by the organization itself but by a specialist firm of consultants – a phenomenon of American commercial life which is now making rapid headway in Britain also.

In the appointment of junior executives the multiple choice test has become the key to the good life. It is so, because it seems to offer a means of by-passing all those unfortunate dilemmas of judgement, of liking and not liking, of appreciating this quality but not that, which arise when one has actually to deal with human beings. Instead it brings, or so it is assumed, to the measurement and analysis of human character and ability, something of the statistical precision that is possible when one is dealing with metals or other inanimate objects whose tensile strength, durability under stress, reaction to extremes of heat and cold and the rest can be measured with certitude.

The making of multiple choice tests has become a flourishing business. According to the Mental Measurements Year Book there are now over 950 tests produced by 173 different organizations. Many of these organizations, according to Professor Banesh Hoffman, a former collaborator of Einstein's at the Institute of Advanced Studies, Princeton, who has recently subjected the whole multiple test procedure to a good deal of sceptical scrutiny, employ travelling salesmen to promote their wares. Their tests are used for increasingly large groups of job candidates in private business. 'Busy executives – especially those who secretly lack confidence in their own judgement – are,' Professor Hoffman remarks, 'only too happy to hand over to professional testers the job of deciding who is worthy and who is not.'

The use of such tests has not yet gone so far in Britain as in America. But under the impact of the American example British business is learning. The Institute of Industrial Psychology and the Tavistock Institute of Human Relations both have rapidly growing lists of British business clients for such services. So do many private management selection organisations. It may soon be as dangerous to put a tick wrong here as in America.

These multiple tests have one great attraction. It is a part of their nature – indeed one might say that it is the essence of their nature – that what they find out can be punched on cards fed into other machines – computers, electronic brains and suchlike master minds of modern society – and can there be persuaded to divulge ever-increasing combinations of information about the man – the human being – who took the test. These can be filed and added to as occasion arises. They provide a permanent mechanical insight into this man – this human being – when any question of promotion or suchlike arises: a passport, if not quite to eternity, to everything short of it.

Moreover, these multiple tests do not require anything so

uncomfortable as imagination or the ability to express ideas on the part of he who is to be tested.

They present the applicant with a number of situations coyly thought up by the test makers – men it would often appear of remarkably opaque minds – to measure his tact, initiative, judgement, emotional maturity and what have you. He may for example, to quote from one much used test, be asked to imagine himself a publisher offered a scholarly and valuable work which he intends to turn down because he cannot see enough chance of making money out of it. He then has to choose which of a number of letters to the author dreamed up by the test maker is best suited 'to inform him of your decision without discouraging him'. Or, to quote another, he may be asked to say which of a number of stated 'assumptions' is made if someone says to you, 'We need to save time in getting there, so we'd better go by plane.' Or, to give a third, which among several suggested courses of action he would take if he saw a woman standing with a baby at the window of a burning house. Or for that matter what of several possible things come into his mind when someone says bed or umbrella or red.

The answers concocted by the tester are marked A B C D... The job applicant reveals himself by his choice. He cannot ask for an explanation if the question seems to him to be obscurely phrased or badly expressed. Nor is he allowed to say why he chose one answer rather than another. All he has to do is tick.

It is possible, of course, that a man of inventive and original mind might, if left to himself, think up quite different answers from any of those offered by the tester or even decide that the questions themselves miss the point. But this, looked at properly, is not a criticism of the tests. Who would want such a man anyway?

On analysing questions used in American multiple choice tests and checking the 'correct' answers against those of men with already established reputations in business, the professions or academic life Professor Hoffman found that many tests 'actually load the dice against you if your ability is far above average.' Some of the test makers admit this. But nothing can be done about it. 'You must,' as Professor Hoffman points out, 'pay a penalty for being exceptional. You are a statistical misfit in an age of mechanized judgement.' Independent thought is not required.

America likes anarchists. But only if they have a lot of money. The young man making a start should think to formula. He should concentrate on ticking wisely. By so doing he may hope to acquire a personality which, when all the scores and sub-scores of the tests are brought together and fed into the right machine, will provide a profile of his character and suitability for employment or promotion that no one thereafter can gainsay – at least no one who believes that the mechanistic approach to life brings home all the answers.

To argue that the flavour of a man of exceptional but idiosyncratic talent or of unconventional approach to life may escape the machine is not a criticism. It does not want him. What the organization requires, particularly the large organization, is men who either already fit the Procrustes' Bed of the multiple tests or can be trimmed to do so and thus become a part of what one important business executive questioned by *Fortune* on how executives make decisions justly described as a 'composite mind' making 'corporate decisions'.

The young man with an ambition to be part of a 'composite mind' – and this after all is what most ambitious young American men do wish to be to judge from the responses of college seniors – had not only better be careful where he puts his ticks but be sure to live up to them afterwards. His future depends on a filing cabinet. Not only must he make sure of getting the right kind of filing card with the right holes punched in to start with, he must not let his card down by doing anything unexpected afterwards.

In a properly organized organization this card of his will keep those above him informed not only of his abilities and his progress in the organization but of his 'degree of sociability' – and his wife's too when he begins to get far enough up for her to matter – his degree of contentment, his degree of dominance, his degree of conservatism, his cultural interest (he should be careful not to have too much of this as it can be a positive disadvantage), whether he reads books and if so what, what comes into his mind when someone says naked, or, maybe, night, and a whole lot of other things that even his nearest and dearest do not know about him.

Naturally, human beings being what human beings are, no organization, however big, expects all its entrants completely to fit its own organization profile when they start. But the good organization does expect that in a matter of two or three years, at most, they will have been smoothed down to come pretty close to it. Those that want to succeed had better let the smoothing be done. What they need to do is to get as close as they can to that organization profile and stick by it. The approved norm brings home the bacon.

His working life will of itself, of course, help the properly adjusted young man to achieve this, just as life in the right suburb will, or, if it comes to that, marriage to the right sort of wife. It will teach him to belong and to think of himself as a member of a team, to be 'well rounded' and believe in group decisions and to be completely aware of his exact place in the hierarchy of the organization.

If he is a member – as a young man so obviously destined for success as he almost certainly will be – of a big organization this latter will be made clear at every stage of his career to him and everyone else by the situation and size of his office, the furnishing of that office, at what stage he gets a water carafe on his desk, and when that desk becomes mahogany instead of oak, which staff dining-room he eats in, what washroom he uses, the situation of his space in the parking lot (if he is sufficiently far up to have a parking space) and the kind of car he runs.

The office will also let him know, informally in most cases but formally in some, how much home entertaining he should do with other members of the staff and which of them. In this matter it is essential not to seek to know socially either anyone much above or much below you in the firm. You should stick to those as nearly as possible of the same rank as yourself. If you, or they, are promoted, then your mutual entertaining should stop – except perhaps for a formal cocktail party. Even on your own level it is wise not to let friendships grow too deep. You should, as *Nation's Business* points out, avoid the 'millstone of personal commitments, loyalties and friendships'.

One way and another, indeed, there is not now much that is permissible for many young or even middle-aged Americans in the way of giving their individualities a run. Perhaps this is why the trade in 'personalized' objects of all sorts is so large: you may find thousands of them in the mail order catalogues alone. The man who buys himself a personalized tie bar or a shirt with his initials on, or a personalized television programme cover, or even a personalized denture dish, may not be doing much to avow his individuality but he is doing something: at least he is asserting the fact that he has an identity.

One suspects, too, that the anonymity of the individual, the merging of the person in the group, is, at lower social levels, the reason for all those rather pathetic name buttons worn by store assistants and others. The organization of the super-market and the self-serve chain store have robbed them of the personality they were once required to exercise in meeting with customers, in the exchange of talk and advice across the counter, in actually selling things. It has left them with nothing but their names – nothing but their names, and the bright synthetic smiles, and the repetition of the same friendly, automatic phrases – 'You're welcome', 'Come and see us again soon' – as they punch the calculating machines, and give you your check and pack your purchase in the big, brown, paper bag, you and all the hundreds of other you's, until no doubt, although the smiles still flash, they could weep with the boredom of it all. But they are still somebody. They have an identity. They are Mamie, or Doris or Kay. It says so on their smart green overalls. It must be true.

10

The Corroding Fear

ONE cannot, if one thinks in human terms about American society, escape McCarthyism – that period so short a time ago when, to quote the words of one of his biographers, Mr. Richard Rovere, McCarthy 'walked with heavy tread over large parts of the Constitution of the United States and cloaked his own gross figure in the sovereignity it asserts and the powers it distributes'. Nor dare one ignore it when one considers the American invasion.

McCarthy is now, of course, old history – although not so very old, only eight years old. It may seem that to revive the sad story of those years is scarcely relevant to the America of the 'sixties and even less so to the impact of American ideas and American ways on Britain. But societies do not change their total character in eight years, nor can anyone say with confidence that although McCarthy is dead McCarthyism is also. The fact of McCarthy is one of the facts, as hard and uncomfortable as a block of granite, that has to be faced with whatever equanimity one can when one tries to reach a true picture of this civilization whose invading forces now press so insistently on our own. One can seek to explain McCarthyism as a mood of passing hysteria, argue that McCarthy would never have been allowed the run he had under a stronger President, say that although he climbed high he did not last long. All this may be true. But one cannot ignore the ecology of human societies. When everything else has been tossed on the table the huge sociological fact remains that he happened, and that he happened in this setting.

It would, of course, be absurd to suggest that to open one's doors to American techniques of salesmanship and credit buying, or even to accept the American dream of upward mobility from plushy suburb to plushier suburb, or the American promise of the satisfying life as one most likely to be found on the conformist executive ladder of a big corporation is to prepare the way for a British McCarthy. Or, for that matter, that the American emphasis (so necessary to the American economy) on talking and behaving and being like one's fellows – a regular guy – necessarily means that those who fall captive to the glossy surface of American material splendour, as it is so easy to do, also inherit the political and social attitudes that McCarthyism exemplified. McCarthyism had deeper roots in the American character and the American past – in that unique experience out of which America with all its glories and anxieties has been born – than are to be found in the mechanics of American civilization as it presents itself to the world today.

Yet it would be no less mistaken not to recognize that the soil in which American consumer civilization of the second half of the twentieth century flourishes – that consumer civilization that we are being asked to embrace – was also the one that nourished McCarthy.

McCarthy did more damage to the good name of America in the world than any other single man in its history. 'In all countries they know of him and in all tongues they speak of him,' said Adlai Stevenson at the end of a world tour in 1953. Yet eight years ago much of American society was lying on its back before this man with its feet in the air like a cowed puppy waiting to be kicked or fondled as he pleased.

How did it happen? How did it come about, as Karl E. Mayer of the *Washington Post*, writing to Richard Rovere asked, that American society appeared so vulnerable to an adventurer 'armed mainly (so it seems) by the timidity of his victims'? Why should there be this softness at the centre of American civilization? Before we copy it we ought to know – if we can.

McCarthy cannot be divorced from his time – and his time was only eight years ago. There have been other moods of hysterical suspicion in American history, as in the history of many other nations. There was one not very dissimilar after the First World War. But never at any previous time in American history has a man such as he been able to exercise so complete and all-pervading an influence over almost every aspect of American life with so little effective opposition to him.

That this should have been so in the full tide of American material plenitude when so much of what seems attractive in American life to so many people in Britain and elsewhere had been achieved is as relevant to a consideration of the American invasion as any of the wealth it carries in its hands. Societies cannot be fragmented into the good and the bad. They are unities. McCarthy's story is, in an important sense, as much a part of the commercialized mass-produced civilization that American business has created with such awe-inspiring energy as any of the gleaming convertibles on the freeways or the electric dishwashers in the kitchens: it is the obverse side of the treasury of the super-markets, the secret writing on the back of the credit cards.

Joseph R. McCarthy, who liked to be called Joe, died in the Naval Medical Centre at Bethesda on 2 May 1957, of an illness aggravated by heavy drinking. He was forty-eight. His power had seeped away before the television cameras three years earlier when a Boston lawyer, Mr. James Linden Welch, the son, one likes to recall with, no doubt, altogether unjustified national pride, of an English housemaid and a rating in the Royal Navy, was goaded in the Army – McCarthy hearings to stand up to him with dry contempt and by his cross-examination reveal to a television-viewing audience that sometimes totalled 20,000,000 just what sort of a man he was, and that he was vulnerable, and by so doing bred courage in others.

McCarthy had begun his public career eighteen years earlier as a circuit Judge in Wisconsin at a salary of $8,000 a year, out of which he saved $50,000 in just under three years. When America entered the war he joined the Marine Corps, although he still held on to his Judgeship, and served in the Pacific for two and a half years, mainly on non-combatant duties, interviewing pilots for intelligence purposes on their return from missions. When he was refused three months' leave of absence at the height of the fighting in the South Pacific to campaign for re-election as a Judge he resigned his commission and returned home. In 1946 he was elected a Republican Senator for Wisconsin, largely on the platform, if such it can be called, that 'Washington needs a Tail Gunner' – which he had never been.

In Washington he became a spokesman for Pepsi-Cola, for building interests opposed to public housing, and for other groups with dollars on offer. By 1950, up to which time he had shown no interest in Communism or any important public issue, he was in trouble with both the Department of Taxation and the Board of Bar Commissioners, and was discredited in his own party.

It was at this stage that he discovered Communism. He was introduced to it over lunch as a useful subject for a Senator with a need to attract notice to himself by a fellow Catholic, Father Edmund A. Walsh, of Georgetown University – who later, when the uses to which his suggestion had been put became clear, felt it necessary to repudiate him.

McCarthy was not the first to play on the American fear of Communism abroad and at home – that fear which cannot help but seem so extravagant to those in Europe who have lived with the danger for a long time and have seen no reason to weaken their own hold on freedom to counter it. The Hiss case had shocked the public. The campaign for a loyalty oath in universities and elsewhere had already begun. But nobody, it soon became plain, could use it like Joe.

Four weeks after his lunch with Father Walsh he started his career as the most successful witch hunter in American history by waving before a gathering of Republican ladies in Wheeling, West Virginia, a piece of paper. On it, he declared, were the names of 205 proven Communist Party members in the State Department. This statement was a lie. The paper was not what he said it was. He had no such names. He produced no evidence. He did not substantiate his charges. At no time, in fact, did he ever produce concrete evidence to substantiate any of the statements that poured out of him in an increasingly vicious torrent of suspicion and abuse as he found that, almost by accident, he had stumbled on a way to get the public ear. He merely picked up bucket after bucket of slime and threw it.

There may have been some Communist agents in the U.S. Government service, just as there proved to be some in the service of other Governments. If there were McCarthy did not find them. The Hiss case had shaken American confidence, but the acts for denying which Algar Hiss was convicted of perjury in 1950 had been committed by him thirteen years before in the entirely different world of the 'thirties. Although the security services had, by this time, been almost over-zealous in their purging of anyone who could be regarded as the slightest security risk; there may still in this year 1950 have been men in positions of trust who ought not to have been where they were. But there is no evidence to show that this was so and if there were any such men McCarthy did not find them.

He did not need to do so. In the United States in the middle of the twentieth century it was, it soon appeared, sufficient to accuse – to accuse anybody and everybody, without discrimination, without evidence, without truth. Looking back it seems incomprehensible. Yet, in fact, he scarcely made one speech that was not wholly founded on invention. Almost every statement he made before the Senate Committees which provided him with his public stage was untrue and most were grotesque also. There was hardly a cross-examination he conducted as Chairman of the Senate Committee on Government Operations – flouting every rule of law and decency and fairness in the process – that was not based on lies. This is plain now as one goes through the record. It could have been plain then – and in many cases it was. This was the emptiest campaign in American political history.

Yet by its means he put most of the Administration of the most powerful democracy in the world in abject terror of him. The Senate, not one member of which a few months before had had the slightest respect for him, crawled before him – 'everyone in the Senate or just about everyone,' says Mr. Rovere, who was there every day, 'was scared stiff of him', and there is no reason to doubt the truth of the judgement. Some of them had reason to be. Several who had dared to cross him and whose hold on their places seemed unassailable found themselves politically ruined and driven from office when his agents had finished their work of spreading reports in their home States that they were 'pro-Communist'. What Joe said the people took – no matter who he said it about.

Senior Ministers, including the Secretary of the Army, indeed particularly the Secretary of the Army, fawned on him, eating their words whenever he told them to. The State Department gave him an undertaking that it would make no diplomatic appointments without clearing them through him. Even Eisenhower – the 'liberator of Europe', the father figure of the nation – did what he was told. To such an extent indeed, and it is surely one of the most discreditable of all the almost incomprehensible events of that time, that when this drunken trickster, whose whole career had been based on lies, described the great soldier and public servant, to whom Eisenhower owed most of his preferment and fame, General Marshall, as 'a traitor steeped in falsehood' and let it be known that any praise of his friend and patron by Eisenhower would be regarded with disfavour, Eisenhower remained silent. Instead, on the platform in Milwaukee from which he had intended to defend his friend, he publicly embraced his accuser.

But McCarthy's power, almost supreme in Washington for four years, ran far beyond the boundaries of Government. Before he was done his influence penetrated almost every industry and business of any size in the country – including especially, but by no means exclusively, the film industry. It moved into State Governments and into the universities. It pervaded the armed services. It touched at one time or another almost every aspect of public and social life in the country, and it ruined the lives of many ordinary people.

Yet when at last opposition did come and the Senate, emboldened by Mr. Welch and the outcome of the Army hearings, called up its courage and passed a vote of censure on him, he collapsed almost overnight, a bladder of a man destroyed by his own moral emptiness.

Even at the height of his success not all Americans agreed with McCarthy and not all those who did not agree with him took cover. Some did. But the number of those who fought him is also relevant.

There were some, like those Faculty members at Berkeley and elsewhere who resigned their posts rather than submit to the inroads on academic independence required of them by a loyalty oath, who were ready to risk their careers rather than give way to fear of McCarthyism. There were many writers and lecturers, like the philosopher, Alexander Meiklejohn, one of the great men of America, who at the age of over eighty is still fighting with unabated energy and courage for the right of all Americans to think and speak and act as their conscience dictates, who did not hesitate to speak out. In the Information Services, the State Department and a few other Governmental Agencies there were some who fought the inroads of McCarthyism with all the power they could command – it was often a very small and lonely power – jeopardizing their professional future rather than fall in with his demands, although those who should have supported them in the White House and Senate cowered before him.

To their credit most of the organized Churches opposed him. So, although heavily under his attack, did most organized Labour. So also did the best of the independent universities. No similar accolade can be claimed for the Press. The newspapers gave the lies of McCarthy the publicity on which he thrived, with the defence that it was their duty to report objectively. They failed, for the most part, to fulfil their other not less important duty of setting the news in perspective and of helping their readers to discriminate between what was true and false. Nevertheless, although more popular newspapers and magazines all over the country than any journalist can think of without shame scuttled into neutrality or actively threw their influence behind the most sordid campaign in American political history, the best of the Press, the *New York Times*, the *New York Herald Tribune*, the *Washington Post*, the Cowles group of newspapers, the Knight newspapers, *Harper's Magazine*, the *Reporter*, and the more reputable newspapers in many great cities never succumbed to the popular fear of him. They opposed him all through. So did the Luce publications.

On the air the best of the commentators attacked him: Edward R. Murrow, Elmer Davis, Martin Agronsky and others. So did most of the leading columnists in print: Walter Lippmann, Marquis Childs, the Alsop Brothers, Drew Pearson. All honour to those, whether in public or private positions, who did what they could to keep alive the civilized virtues in a difficult time.

But the fact remains that for four years he was permitted to bestride the American scene like a demagogic Mephistopheles whose poison spread into every nook and cranny, not only of public activity but of mass entertainment, advertising, business and industry and social life. The fact that some institutions and individuals, although few politicians directly dependent on popular support, dared to oppose him, and that some of them were of great public eminence and influence, does not diminish the significance of this. On the contrary it heightens it.

'Nobody loves Joe but the People,' they used to sing at his meetings and the American people, and the kind of society they have created, must bear the responsibility.

At the height of his campaign fifty per cent of all Americans had, on the evidence of opinion polls, a 'favourable impression' of him. What is in some ways even more significant is that the fifty per cent who did not, made no real attempt to resist him; indeed more than a third of them either felt it safer to have 'no opinion' or actually had none. It is not the wickedness of McCarthy that appals. The pages of history are full of evil men. It is the supineness of the society in which he operated.

The technique by which McCarthy built the fantastic neo-Gothic edifice of his political power was that of the multiple lie. Lie was piled on lie with so wild an abandon, the proliferation of untruth spread so far, the jungle of falsehood became so impenetrable, that it may well be that it was hard at first to believe that there was nothing there. It may well be, also, that there was that in the character and appearance of McCarthy that had a nostalgic appeal for some of his fellow countrymen. In the age of the administration man, of the politician groomed for stardom by public relations officers with every wrinkle and rumple rubbed out, of an America in which many ordinary people felt themselves more and more the captives of the big machine, he, at any rate, was not just another model off the assembly line.

He made no concessions to respectability. On the contrary by some quirk of demagogic intuition he went out of his way to affront all the respectable virtues. His hard drinking, the obscenity of his language, his heavy pawing of any women who came near him, the boorishness of his manners as he belched his way through conversation, the crumpled condition of his dress. the shadow on his chin – all these were notorious, for he saw to it that they were. He was a figure from America's past – this swilling, swearing, poker-playing roughneck, lurching into the committee room from an all-night stag session, who fought to cripple, and to hell with the rules; the poor boy from Wisconsin bucking the top brass; the man who didn't give a damn for office and did not want it: the broken anarchist at the heart of American life.

To some extent, also, what was written of a much greater man, and a much more talented artist in the music of demagogy was true of him: 'One catches in his company that flavour of final purposelessness, inner irresponsbiility, existence outside or away from our Saxon good and evil, mixed with cunning, remorselessness, love of power, that lent fascination, enthralment and terror to the fair seeming magicians of North European folklore.' This Irish Catholic from the farmlands of Outagamie County, Wisconsin, had little of the charm and fascination of Lloyd George, none of his magic in speech or wisdom in statesmanship. But it is not altogether absurd to see in him a vulgarized version of the 'goat-footed, half-human visitor from the hag-ridden woods of Celtic antiquity' that Maynard Keynes saw in the Welshman. Such men attract power by the very unpredictability of their motives.

Yet when all this is said the mystery remains. If he was in some sense a figure from America's past he was also an omen of its present. Neither his gifts, nor his lying, nor his sense of timing could have brought him the power he had if there had not been something empty at the heart of modern America to respond to the emptiness and destructiveness that was in him. No doubt the liar in a position of trust has always some initial advantage in a civilized society: civilized societies are natural suckers for the myth that there is no smoke without fire. But the lies McCarthy told were from the very first so outrageous that they could only have been believed, even momentarily, in a sick society.

To believe McCarthy meant believing that most of the men at the head of national affairs were fools or rogues or both. It meant believing that a man like Marshall was a traitor. It meant believing you could trust no one.

Millions of Americans were apparently prepared to believe this. This is the shattering fact about American society that one cannot ignore. It cannot be explained by the flaw in McCarthy. It can only be explained by the flaw in American society.

In the end this disbelief went far beyond the confines of Government. All over this vast country Americans were prepared to believe that their society was so demoralized and the virtues it inculcated so superficial that it was impossible to be sure of the loyalty of anyone, even those you had known or worked with for years.

And after all, when it came down to it, who in this rootless, mobile society with its constantly shifting population on the way up, its belief in the easy ride and its contempt for the human fidelities of the past, who did you know? You didn't know anyone. Not really to know. 'Hi, fellow,' you said, and you had yourselves a good time with the crowd, and you talked the same words and went to the same ball games and agreed that business was tough and, maybe, you even worked in the same organization. But when it came right down to it there was no one you really knew.

In this empty loneliness America listened to the voice of McCarthy and looked over its shoulder. Never have the people of a great nation written themselves down so low on the say-so of one man.

And so it happened that again and again, not only in Government service but in industry, business and the professions, a whispered allegation, nearly always totally irrelevant, usually wholly baseless, sometimes founded on mistaken identity, could destroy a man's livelihood – often with not one among those he had thought his friends willing even to tell him why, or speak a word in his defence lest to do so should bring upon them the taint of suspicion by association. Not all, of course, were silent. Not all sat when the courage to stand up and be counted in another's defence was needed. If there was demoralization it did not hold everyone in its grip. But how many it did hold. How many it must have held to make McCarthyism possible.

To cling to one's status and one's job. To hang on to one's salary and keep up one's credit payments. To hold one's place in the right group and keep the right label. These, it seemed, had become more important to a great many Americans than principle, or honour, or friendship, or personal loyalty; not to risk being smeared the only virtue. In a society which seemed itself to have lost purpose the primary purpose by which all other purposes were to be judged had become self-preservation.

It was not just the fear of Communism that gave McCarthy his power, although this provided him with his opportunity and his theme. There was an even more corroding fear: the fear of standing against the stream, of being suspected of being unsound, of being tabbed with the wrong label. The fear of the junior executive of his boss, of his ambitious wife of what the leader of local society would think, of both of the disapproval of their crowd. The fear of being an individual and of being alone.

It would be pleasant to forget these years. But for anyone who loves America it is not easy to forget. They made a nonsense of so much there was to admire. The rule of McCarthy did not last long. Only four years. But the fact that it happened, that it could happen, is there. It did not happen anywhere else. Not in Britain, nor France, nor in Canada just across the border. Yet if the provocation existed in the United States it existed not less in any of these.

It is not possible to forget that fact. This, whether one likes it or not, is one of the ingredients that has to be taken into account in any final computation of the qualities – so admirable in so many ways – of that American way of life that now presses so insistently upon us.

11

The Falling Shutter

IT would be pleasant to think that the America of the 'sixties is
wholly purged of McCarthyism. It is, however, difficult to
believe so. On the contrary, during five months there in the first
half of 1961 people of many different professions and backgrounds continuously warned me that it remained a present
danger. It would, they insisted, be altogether mistaken to think
that because McCarthy himself was dead the conditions in
American society that had made his power possible did not
still exist. Or that some of the forces that sheltered behind and
used him when he was alive were not still active now he was
dead.

Even in the first glow of the Kennedy victory before it was
dimmed by the Cuban invasion there was, in fact, already a good
deal of independent evidence that this was so. After Cuba there
was more.

The difficulty for an Englishman in trying to determine how
important this post-McCarthyism is, is that he is at first likely to
find it frankly impossible that anyone could take seriously the
organizations, activities and opinions to which his attention is
drawn. Can anyone, he asks himself, really believe the John Birch
Society, the Christian Anti-Communism Crusade, the Christian
Crusade, the National Education Programme and other similar
bodies of, as it seems to him, crack-pot characters whose propa-
ganda reads like the correspondence of vicious ageing spinsters
with hallucinations; can anyone believe that these are a threat to

anything or anybody, or that the things they say are likely to influence public opinion to any measurable extent? One might as well be expected to take the Empire Loyalists seriously.

The answer, unfortunately, is that not only do many people whose opinions are to be respected take the danger seriously, but that such is the vulnerability of quite considerable groups of American people to any suggestion that 'thousands of Communists are in high places in the United States' that they may well be right in doing so.

All of these organizations have increased substantially in membership and financial backing in the last three years. Between 1957 and 1959 the annual budget of one of the most extreme of these witch-hunting organizations, the Christian Anti-Communism Crusade, rose from a mere $63,000 to $380,000. Contributions to its funds are reported to have more than doubled again in 1960. They were expected to be more than $1,000,000 in 1961.

One of the activities of this particular body is to organize permanent community groups to uncover Communists in their neighbourhoods and keep tabs on all suspected liberals. It is headed by a Dr. Fred C. Swartz, who, while I was there, was attracting audiences all over the country – he claims, almost certainly correctly, to address on average at least three hundred groups a year – by describing in some detail how Communist agents, sheltered by men high in Government, 'will come for you, as they have for many others, and on a dark night, in a dark cellar, take a wide-bore revolver with a soft bullet and place it at the nape of your neck'.

All this, to the innocent English visitor, tends to appear both lunatic and ludicrous when he first comes across it. It tends still to seem so when he hears that Dr. Swartz has been invited to lecture before the Texas legislature – Texas after all is Texas. It becomes less so, however, when he discovers that Dr. Swartz has also been invited to speak to the National War College and that a number of high-ranking Army and Navy officers have presided over community meetings and 'seminars' conducted by him.

The John Birch Society, which takes its name from a missionary who is alleged, without many supporting facts, to have met a hero-martyr's death in China organizing a far-flung resistance to Chinese Communism and is so right wing that it has even accused Mr. Eisenhower of being a Communist, specializes in the organization of clandestine vigilantes groups in the Universities and State Colleges. These groups, which have already put down roots among students in a considerable number of colleges, are instructed to report any 'liberal' tendencies on the part of Professors and students and see that their names and acts are carefully recorded. The John Birch Society also specializes in organizing letter-writing campaigns to newspapers, a field in which it has had a good deal of success. Under the guidance of Robert Welch, owner of a candy and drug store fortune, it has spent large sums and much energy recruiting members in the richer suburbs and townships.

An English investigator finds it difficult to take it seriously – until he remembers McCarthy. But there is plenty of evidence that its funds, its membership and its 'intelligence service' are all growing. Its wilder attacks on Eisenhower and others and its attempt to sow suspicion in local communities have brought counter-attacks from some citizens' groups and local newspapers. Surprisingly, however, one finds a good deal of feeling that such newspapers may be running considerable risks and deserve credit for their courage.

When I was lecturing at the University in Santa Barbara, a rich Southern Californian town and the family home of Mr. Herter, the former Secretary of State, I could not help but notice in a public restaurant where my wife and I had dinner with a group of leading local intellectuals that several of those present carefully dropped their voices and looked over their shoulders to see if anyone was listening when I brought up the subject of the activities of the John Birch Society. However, I am glad to say that the Assistant Publisher of the local newspaper, a tough, attractive character whom I had previously met when he was serving with the American Navy during the war, would have none of this, and raising his voice, proclaimed for the benefit of everyone within earshot that his paper, which had created much excitement by a bold attack on the John Birch Society, would Keep on Keeping after them.

The National Education Programme, whose head is a college president, Dr. George Program, of Harding College in Arkansas, has had startling success in getting its films and literature adopted by school boards across the country. The largest number of its clients are in Texas and Southern California, both parts of the United States much given to the wilder lunacies. But its penetration of the school system is by no means confined to these areas. Several of its films and film strips propounding the thesis that there is a 'left wing fifth column seeking to destroy American democracy and private enterprise' are being used by Junior and Senior High Schools in districts normally considered fairly level-headed.

All these organizations concentrate much of their attack, as does also Christian Crusade, on 'intellectuals' – especially from Harvard. All campaign continuously against public libraries said to contain 'Communist' or 'liberal' books, and against Colleges and High Schools said to have members of staff 'soft on Communism': sometimes it would appear as though to read or think anything at all is in itself and of its nature 'Un-American'.

Even more disturbing in some ways is the backing given by several big corporations and financial institutions to such activities as the film *Operation Abolition*. This film – as was made plain during the hearing of a riot charge against a student who was triumphantly acquitted – deliberately distorted the facts about a largely spontaneous and somewhat ramshackle student protest against the perambulating House Un-American Activities Committee during one of its hearings in San Francisco, in order to try to persuade the American people that the protest was part of a carefully planned Communist plot to destroy American institutions.

What was most frightening was not the doctoring of the evidence – bad though that was – but the fact that much of the film's support came from honest people who automatically assumed that there could have been no protest unless the protestors were, in fact, the hirelings or dupes of Communists.

In such an atmosphere dissent – any dissent – is of itself a proof of guilt.

Nor are there lacking several rather more coy but equally financially well-provided-for bodies which, aided by professional public relations' outfits of the lusher kind, devote themselves to the task of persuading Americans that any man or woman faintly tinged with liberal principles – somewhat to the right shall one say of Mr. Butler or even Mr. Enoch Powell – is either a Communist or 'soft on Communism'.

The same atmosphere ferments a good deal of social life. I recall one house-party at which a charming Hungarian guest, now a naturalized American, who had escaped from Hungary after great risks and sacrifices in fighting the worst of Communist tyranny there, dared to say that she felt that a part of her would always remain European. On hearing this statement, the wife of a rich State Senator turned upon the Hungarian and, almost spitting with venom, screamed at her, 'Go back to Europe then, you Communist. We don't want people like you here. If you don't like America get back where you came from.' When the Hungarian lady, who bore herself with considerable dignity throughout this unprovoked assault, had moved away, only one of the Americans present seemed to think it necessary to speak up on her behalf. No one answered him. They were too concerned fussing around that embodiment of charm and true patriotism, the Senator's lady.

No one in their senses, of course, would indict a community because of the bad manners of one rich, over-fed, middle-aged bitch. But what is more disturbing is the extent to which one finds in the same social groups an almost complete close-down on discussion of anything capable of being construed by the most suspicious and unbalanced mind as 'dangerous thinking'. One gets in such groups – how odd that it should be so – a curious whiff of that same fear of ideas that one has grown accustomed to in Communist societies.

This is not true of all groups. It is not true of most of the writers, journalists and university people one meets – although it is of some of the less able or more ambitious of the latter, with a careful eye on what the 'good people' in the Administration are likely to be thinking. But to touch on what would be regarded as the most commonplace subjects of discussion in any reasonably intelligent English society in the presence of many younger American business and professional men, radio and television executives, advertising men, rising local politicians and others who have their way to make in the world, is to be conscious of a shutter falling.

Nor, despite a welcome resurgence of dissent on many university campuses, can one help but be aware of the existence of the same anxieties in many young people – especially the ambitious ones; the student office holders, the young men 'most likely to succeed'. Already, while still so young, they are armoured against thought in the safe clichés of authority. To talk to them is as unrewarding an experience as to talk to a young Communist from behind the Iron Curtain, and in many ways very similar. One stubs one's toes on a closed mind. Indeed, I had the opportunity one day during a visit of an official Soviet group to the States of lunching with a Russian Youth Leader on one side of me and the President of the Students' Union of a great American university on the other. It was like alternately switching on two gramophones.

This is not universally true of course. To talk, as I had the honour of doing, to a crowd of close on four thousand students at the time of the Cuban invasion, was to be made shiningly aware of the idealism and entirely honourable anxieties of very many American young people. I had the same experience of other campuses when students clustered round me after a lecture on foreign affairs. But for most of the ambitious young it is discretion that counts.

It is possible to enjoy better conversation in America than almost anywhere in the world if you know the right people. (Although sometimes you are likely to feel that you are engaged in a conspiracy while you do so.) But it is also possible to be more unutterably bored there than almost any place on earth.

One's hosts could not be nicer. Their friends are charming as well as rich. The house itself is delightful. The drink is plentiful.

But there is nothing at all to talk about. One leans back with one's glass in one's hand and tries desperately to think of something safe and neutral to say. But there is nothing.

One sometimes has this same feeling in English country houses. But there it is not of the refusal to think but of the inability to do so that one is aware. Comfortable silence and an occasional grunt are all that are expected. Boredom creeps up one's spine like a warm bath.

Here, however, boredom is brittle. The picnic is marvellous, but it is in a public park. The keep-off-the-grass notices confront you at every turn. The shouts and screams rise higher but the invisible attendant is watching. One false step and out you go. You have a mad longing to do something desperate like dropping a tiny piece of litter on the grass: no more than a crumpled scrap of an idea. But when the moment comes you stuff it shame-facedly in your pocket instead. They are all such nice people. How can one embarrass them by saying anything that matters? 'Yes,' you say, 'I love being in America.' 'Well, isn't that won-derful,' they reply, 'what say we all drink up and go some place?'

Dear hospitable, warm-hearted, nervous people, how much I like you; how much I wish so many of you did not seem to think all thought dangerous. How did you ever come to let yourselves be persuaded that it was?

Even in those societies dedicated traditionally to the traffic in ideas one is often conscious of how low the threshold of tolerance is that divides one from the world outside, how perishable the licence to think. A suspicious ear as at the keyhole. The stone-throwers are waiting outside the window.

'Our responsibility,' remarked Dr. Clerk Kerr, President of the University of California, when some members of the State Congress roared with anguish because a group of students had invited a young man awaiting committal to prison on a contempt charge for pleading the First Amendment to speak on the campus at Berkeley, 'Our responsibility is to make students safe for ideas not ideas safe for students.' A simple enough belief one would have thought; little more, indeed, than an academic cliché. But what anger it evoked. In the eyes of several State congressmen and businessmen, Dr. Kerr might as well have been plotting the overthrow of the United States Constitution. 'The business of America,' screamed a maddened columnist in the *San Francisco Chronicle*, 'is to clear out Kerr and all his fellow Communists.'

The columnist in question was a man with an inherited private income, a Rolls-Royce, and a lush taste in evening attire. The following week he was propounding the thesis that most of America's troubles came from a jelly-backed unwillingness to let the police shoot to kill. It hardly seemed possible that anyone could care what such an individual said. But the odd thing was that they did. No one, of course, took seriously his dirty little boy's shriek of 'Communist'. But there it was. It was on the record. Some day, somehow, somewhen, somebody might pick it up again, a green thought in a green shade waiting to be plucked.

One perceived that a statement likely to be regarded as embarrassingly sententious at a degree day in any small provincial university in England – or for that matter at a Y.M.C.A. prize-giving – did, in California in mid-twentieth century, involve a declaration of principle. It was discussed as such at liberal-minded dinner-parties. Listening, one perceived that at this time and place it was not a truism but a heartening gesture of academic freedom by a man of courage and learning.

That an ageing gentleman with a red carnation in his button-hole should subsequently scream Communist in the *San Francisco Chronicle* is no matter for particular remark. Or that others of the same kidney agreed with him. Ageing gentlemen are doing the same thing daily all over the world; Lord Winterton, it will be recalled, once announced that he smelt Communists whenever he walked into the B.B.C.

It was not the remark but the reaction to the remark that was significant — the anxiety, the low-voiced discussions and worried headshakes among those closest to and most admiring of Dr. Clark Kerr, their perturbation lest at some future date it might be recalled and damage him, their relief and pleasure when the Governor of the State of California was persuaded that it was right and expedient to support him and to say, not without controversy, that even the Administration felt it proper for students to be exposed to ideas.

It was as though when Lord Winterton smelled Communists in the B.B.C. there had been, instead of a gale of laughter, anxious deliberations on how best to defend the then Director-General of the B.B.C. and present Editor of *The Times*, Sir William Haley, against future consequences.

Like all democracies, America thrived in the past on controversy. As in all democracies, its leaders often claim that what distinguishes their society is the freedom to say what one pleases. Of course. Of course. But why, one sometimes asks oneself, do not more people seem to want to take advantage of it?

British justice, it was once said, is open to everybody – like the Ritz. One sometimes has the feeling that freedom of opinion in America is equally open to all – except those with their eye on promotion. In the new suburbs it is conformity that makes the grade: the conformity of the women's clubs and the junior Chambers of Commerce, of the glossy magazines and the television screens, so carefully purged – except at the most inconvenient times – of that minimum of dangerous thought that still manages to find its way on to British television.

In the house which we rented when we were last living in America there were three television sets; two black-and-white and one coloured. At the turn of any one of their three knobs one could bring into one's home a choice of some of the most expensive entertainment programmes in the world from I forget how many stations. We did not, in fact, do so very often, for after we had experimented a little it scarcely seemed worth while. One began to have the uncomfortable feeling that one was living in a country whose inhabitants – or at any rate those with television sets – had entered on a self-denying ordinance against thinking. Or perhaps it is only that those who sponsor all these magnificently produced programmes have come to the common conclusion that thought is inimical to the business of persuading people to buy – just as their British counterparts have begun to do.

Perhaps it is the same concern that makes so many American newspapers so dull. They were not always so. The tradition of the radical crusading small-town newspaper editor and publisher is a long and honourable one in American society. It seems to be dying on its feet, if it is not already dead. Today what impresses one most about these small-town newspapers is not their boldness but their blandness. They have become the eunuchs of journalism.

The American Press has been called many names in its past: vulgar, sensational, mud-raking, ruthless – it is sad to see so much of it sinking into a middle age of bland conformity, a defensive social neutrality which robs it of bite and excitement and hands it, gagged and bound, to an all-pervading dullness of negative virtues.

But the Press after all is but the mirror of the age in which it functions. One had never thought to find American society declining into dullness. On many levels of experience and interest such an idea is still absurd. Yet the horrid thought remains that many of the influences most active in American life are directed to producing just this – a bland emptiness, an eroding dullness at the heart of all that magnificent energy.

How strange if the real enemy of America should prove to be, not those external ideologies of which it has been so often warned, and is on the whole so well-equipped to meet, but just plain, old-fashioned, home-grown boredom.

12

How Much American?

How far is Britain likely to go along the American road? The physical extent of the American invasion is already considerable – certainly far more so in many significant areas of industry and business than is commonly realized. And it is increasing rapidly year by year.

But how far has the character of British life itself been Americanized and how far is it likely to become so in the future: Americanized not simply in terms of the American myth, potent as it is, but of the reality of American society which differs from the myth in so many respects?

The surface influence of American ideas, American methods, American conceptions of the good life is already vast and far reaching. We borrow from America without pause.

We learnt opinion polls from America and market testing and consumer research. Many of our advertising techniques, from new modes of advertising design to the sales jingles on commercial television, came to us from across the Atlantic. So did the concepts of persuasion that have set in motion the proliferating army of public relations men.

The canned goods and deep-freeze vegetables, the fish fingers and frozen chip potatoes for the cosy meal at home, the television dinners of potatoes, mushed-up vegetables and cooked meat in gravy, frozen dead and waiting to be thawed out on a plastic plate – surely the most appalling of all American inventions though the one, significantly enough, especially picked for praise by the American Secretary for Agriculture when he opened an exhibition of American food in London; which just shows you what can happen to a civilization – the barbecue restaurants and steak houses that have become the fashion for easy dining-out, all these give many of our eating habits an American trade mark. (The owner of one chain of chicken barbecue restaurants explained to me with great pride that not only were the chickens bred to exactly the same size so that each portion would be the same and could be delivered to the customer's table with the maximum of machine-like efficiency, but even the chairs were specially designed to become increasingly uncomfortable for those who dallied too long at table and interfered with the rate of turnover.)

A sizeable number of comic strips – including the new intellectual ones – that we read or do not read in our newspapers are imported or largely derived from American models.

We have taken to bowling alleys and Go Kart races. The juke box pours its noise hardly less raucously on the British than the American air.

We are even beginning to introduce canned music – played softly for relaxed living – in some of our new office blocks. The super-markets, too, are developing it – romantic music produces among shoppers, it has been found in America, a sense of well-being and release from the more mundane claims of reality that has very satisfactory results on their buying. If there, why not here?

The teen-age world is predominantly American. This is very natural. It is an American invention – like Mothers' Day. No one had ever thought of those between the ages of fifteen and nineteen as a specific social group until the Americans invented the term thirty years ago. It remained not much more than a name until after the war, when it occurred to sale-promotion specialists that here was something to be exploited – a new buying group which, if it could be given a sense of identity and cohesion, would bring money to those who catered for it.

Teen-age music, teen-age clothes, teen-age drinks, teen-age amusements are mainly American inspired (although some

British teen-agers are growing out of them and turning to Italian and Continental models and the H. bomb has done the American image some harm among the politically minded among them) for the very good reason that the whole conception began as a piece of creative advertising to exploit the potential High School market in a more organized way.

The teen-age idols are mostly the same on both sides of the Atlantic – first and most potent of them, James Dean, 'The Rebel Without a Cause', whose death masks are still on sale in London and whose fans six years after his death are scarcely less numerous than they were when he was alive, as the revival of his early film, *East of Eden*, showed. Other idols, some of them British, have risen since of course. But even when the nationality changes the climate remains the same. And it is basically an American climate. Understandably so. More British teen-agers may have been influenced by the beat generation than know anything about it but the physical mobility of American life of which the restless wanderings of the original beatniks were a part – the sense of a place where you can pile into a second-hand automobile with the crowd or thumb a ride from a truck-driver and put a thousand miles between yourself and your roots, is very satisfying to the restless ethos of the teen-age world with its international American language, Jazz.

The magazines teen-agers read, like their clothes and hair styles, are all heavily influenced by America. *A Dream Come True* proclaims the most successful of the magazines for teen-age girls, *Honey*, announcing a series in which a young actress, Valerie Pitt, with 'a one-way ticket and a few pounds to tide her over' tells of her adventures in New York.

'I was met,' Valerie records breathlessly, 'by this friend in a glamorous red-and-white Buick Convertible ... That's when the pace started to hot up, and who am I to complain. I just gave myself up to this crazy city.' She meets a friend of Perry Como and then Perry Como himself – 'He told me he loved London teen-agers.' And next day, 'Some guy drove me all over the city – the Bowery, Harlem, Chinatown and then to the Tower Suite (very exclusive) for cocktails.' Broadway, 'it makes Piccadilly

Circus look like something out of a puppet show,' and a party in Greenwich Village, 'very wild', and American men: 'They really *do* cherish their women, be it wife or girl-friend. A woman over here is a success symbol and something very necessary.' Wonderful, wonderful American world in which, 'Teenagers have a marvellous time. They begin dating very young and never have to be home before 2 a.m.'

If the teen-age world, with its American insistence on the impossibility of any understanding between the generations, is largely American created (which is not to say there would not have been Teddy-boys or adolescent violence in our anxious post-war world without it: there would) much of that more-adult society into which the teen-ager moves as a 'young married' is also increasingly oriented to this same vivid transatlantic dream. The architecture, the furniture styling, the flower arrangements, the menus and the fiction featured in the most popular of the women's magazines all tend to have an American flavour: even when the serials and short stories are not bought from America, their social assumptions are the same. The modern young British mother, like the American, brings up her children the Spock way, doing nothing that will upset the most widely read Professor in the world – Dr. Benjamin Spock of Cleveland, Ohio whose "Baby and Child Care", has sold over 14,000,000 copies.

We have not yet wholly adopted the surburban American world of total credit. But the hire purchase debt in Britain now amounts to over £900,000,000 and but for recurring Government credit restrictions it would undoubtedly be much higher. As it is the percentage of British housewives owning electric washing machines, most of them bought on credit, has doubled in the last five years and those owning refrigerators trebled: the purchase both of electric sewing machines and steam irons has gone up two and a half times. The 'Californian Kitchen' featured in the home-making magazines is still a good way from reality for most of their readers. But it represents a dream that becomes steadily more potent.

'Businesses can only survive,' says the Chairman of the Market Development Co., Mr. Bernard Falk in a widely used book on

The Business of Management which draws heavily on American experience, 'if those responsible for them realize that what they think they produce – whether goods or services – is of less importance than what the consumer thinks he or she is consuming.' What a very large number of British consumers now think they are consuming, or at the very least expect to be consuming soon, are those lovely American material possessions they read about so regularly in their magazines and see even more regularly on films and television.

Like the distinguished Editor of the *Christian Science Monitor*, Mr. Erwin Canham, many Americans deplore 'the tawdry materialism of conspicuous consumption spread by the mass media, accompanied by rock 'n roll, splattered by comic books . . . (which) has become the symbol of America in most of the world'. But it is a symbol both potent and agreeable to many in Britain today.

It is to America that much of British business turns as it seeks guidance on how best to adapt itself to the opportunities of the second half of the twentieth century.

In questions of staff selection and what has come to be called, in one of those incredible phrases it is *de rigueur* to use in management consultancy, 'worker motivation', in T.W.I. (which means, initials are mandatory, Training Within Industry), in Job Methods and Job Relations, in Executive Development Programmes and all such matters, it is from American experience (as well as the American language) that British business borrows.

There are still, of course, those who cannot bring themselves to go all the way. 'A striking feature of some American programmes for executive development,' observes Mr. Falk in his book on management, 'is the participation of the psychologist. There is considerable use and experimentation in psycho-analytic techniques for the appraisal of personality and motivation not only in the initial recruitment of staff but also in the periodic appraisals of experienced managers and in the 'diagnostic study' of their relations with, and adjustment to, their environment'. He adds, however, that many British managements are not yet ready to accept these without suspicion. No doubt they will learn in time.

No such reluctance exists towards most other American practices. One American technique which is now being successfully promoted here by a consulting firm is known as 'Management Strategy'. Potential 'top managers' are set theoretical problems in marketing, budgeting or manufacturing. Their decisions are watched over by a specially programmed electronic computer. As each decision is made the computer analyses it and gives judgement on whether it would bring success or disaster. Like the editor's the computer's decision, no doubt, is final.

British management is still less stratified than American. But here, too, American influence is making itself felt. Status symbols have become almost as important in some British firms as in America, the hierarchial structure scarcely less rigid. When reductions in the size of the Services made the number and nature of the opportunities likely to be available in business for officers axed in mid-career a matter of public interest I talked, during the making of a B.B.C. television programme, to Army and Naval officers who had already moved into industry. How difficult, I asked them, had they found it to adjust to the competitiveness of business life?

To my surprise I found that it was not competition that troubled most of them – especially in the newer industries modelled on American operations – but the industrial hierarchy. This they found much more subtle and extensive both in and out of the office than anything they had known in the services. Several who had jobs in new industries in the Midlands said that although they themselves had in time got used to protocol within the works and now knew not to sit at the wrong table in the wrong dining-room, use a lavatory above their station in life, or express an opinion without first being asked to do so by someone at the right level, they found social life outside the factory very difficult. Their wives, they said, found it even more so and were so constrained by the unwritten rules of the company as to who on the firm you could and could not entertain at home that social life in residential areas where most people were employed by the same organization tended to be meagre.

'In the Army,' one of them said, 'you knew exactly where

you were. When you were on duty there was a clearly defined chain of command, but in the mess you mixed up together and if your wife liked a fellow's missus you didn't have to spend your time worrying whether he was a captain and you were a major or the other way round. But here your level determines your life outside the factory as well as in. It makes social life for your wife hell.'

This appears to be a new phenomenon in British industrial life. It certainly did not exist in the industrial areas in the North which I knew in my youth. But it is frighteningly like the pattern in many small American communities round a large industrial unit.

So, too, is the importance now assumed by the motor-car: Jaguars for the Managing Director (unless it is a very big firm, when it will be a Bentley, and a Rolls for the Chairman), Humbers next, and so on down the staff ranks. I know of one instance where a high-up girl secretary with a passion for motoring was left a pleasantly sizeable legacy by an aunt and proceeded to fulfil a long-cherished dream by buying herself an Alvis in which she drove proudly to the works. Next day she was summoned to the Personnel Director's office and told that she would have to choose between the car and the job. An Alvis was not for secretaries.

In many more subtle and less tangible ways the American invasion advances. It would be unfair to blame on America the remarkable manifestation of total lack of interest in anything but the ability to buy more that many observers claim to have found among a large number of electors at the last General Election. But the affluent consumer-society, of which America presents so much the most outstanding example in the world's history, develops its own ethos – its own built-in set of value judgments. Many of these are alien to the traditional character of the British people – although it cannot be denied that they seem to like them. This does not necessarily make them immoral. Tradition is not sacrosanct. But if we are going to develop new social values it would be nice if they were at least our own, not imported ones.

So far British society is a good way from being an identical copy of American. Indeed, returning home after a long stay in the United States, one is likely to be most struck by how un-American much British life still manages to be. It is only as one looks closer that one sees the extent to which Americanism is taking over: how much we have come to regard it as our national fate.

The B.B.C. does not give as much of its top viewing time to American programmes as commercial television does: some $3\frac{1}{4}$ to $3\frac{3}{4}$ hours a week at peak times compared with $7\frac{3}{4}$ to $8\frac{1}{4}$ hours – excluding such programmes as 'What's My Line?', 'This Is Your Life' and 'Candid Camera' where the idea comes from America and is paid for on a royalty basis. But where it felt it necessary to try to find an answer to commercial television's home grown 'Emergency Ward 10' it at once turned across the Atlantic and bought an American hospital serial. Ask yourself if you can imagine American television screens featuring a British hospital serial week by week. This is what the relationship between the two of us has now become.

To deplore the adoption of all American methods or ignore the substantial advantages the flow of American capital and American ideas has brought to some sectors of industry would be absurd. But the main force of the invasion in terms of capital investment, management participation and the influence of American consumer values on our domestic lives as a consequence of television advertising, pop records and the wider distribution of popular American writing (including all those books on how to adjust to yourself, make friends with your boss, and learn to be a social success) through the enormous expansion in paperback distribution, has only come in the last ten years. Ten years is not long in the life of a nation. Yet already some of the consequences of this invasion are profound.

Do we – especially when we look beyond the American myth to the reality of American life today – want them to grow?

13

Point of Decision

ON the first page of his excellent – although often wrong-headed – book, *The British* (wrong-headed to me no doubt in much the same way as much that I have written about the Americans will seem wrong-headed to him), Mr. Drew Middleton, the Chief London Correspondent of the *New York Times*, remarks that one of the first of the paradoxes one encounters in studying the British people is that although homogeneity in basic political thought seems far greater in Britain than in the United States, the resistance to standardization is much more stubborn.

So indeed it is – a fact that sometimes misleads the foreign visitor into thinking the gulfs between classes and regional groups larger than they actually are: the reason the British do not talk or behave like each other is often not because they are prevented from doing so by some invisible but powerful barrier but very simply because they do not want to.

This dislike of standardization is, I conceive, one of the best of the British qualities. It would be sad to see it diminish. Yet it is inimical to much that Americanization has to offer – and to offer, very often, in return for quite substantial material advantages which depend on an increasing number of people being willing to behave in the same way.

A certain amount of standardization is, of course, unavoidable. Even if we wanted to we could not resist it and keep solvent. Nor would anyone in their senses want to. It is the only practical way of making available to large numbers of people what crafts-manship and private patronage formerly produced at high cost for a few. Similarly, one cannot expect to have mass entertainment in films and radio and television and the press – with all the opening of windows on many once dark and stuffy parlours of the mind it has brought – without paying the bill in a greater standardization of some ideas and attitudes.

So far, as Mr. Middleton says, standardization has spread less wide and gone less deep in British than American society. It is still, so to speak, on the surface, accepted in terms of practical advantage but external to the emotional and intellectual values which mainly influence our lives.

What American experience suggests, however, is that if the pressures towards standardization – standardization of production, standardization of consumption, standardization of executive and administrative practices – are permitted to gain too great a hold on a society then it is exactly such an intrusion into intellectual and emotional life that is to be feared. A point of decision is reached. You come to a stage where if you want all that a completely unfettered deployment of the resources of modern civilization can offer in the satisfaction of material appetites you must be prepared to pay the price. It is no longer enough to use conformity as a practical tool. You must be ready to recreate yourself in its image.

I do not suggest that America has yet gone irrevocably beyond this point of decision. Powerful forces of opposition to conformity still exist there. But I do not think it is easy to deny that a good deal of American society has moved close to it. Nor can one avoid the sense of the speed of the progression that hits one on a return to America after an absence of some years.

We are still a good way farther off than America from that point. But some of the forces that are driving America towards it have penetrated deep into Britain in the last ten years.

It is probably true that the complete Americanization of any country other than America itself is impossible. The United States is the product of an experience too unique to be duplicated. The real danger lies in the partial and piecemeal taking over of more and more aspects of American life, either because American investment and American salesmanship in search of fringe markets persuade us to do so, or because we are so beglamoured by the American wave of the future that we accept more of America than it is possible for our society to assimilate and still remain true to its own virtues.

There are, of course, some things American that are capable of being transplanted. But there are others that are not. Even those that are need to be given time to put down roots and adapt themselves to the change of climate. Too facile a transplantation can produce, at the best, no more than an inferior version of the original – just as when one goes into one of the new super-markets that are springing up so rapidly all over suburban England what often strikes one is not the likeness to America but the extent to which the slickness and efficiency, the vigour and exuberance of the original have been lost in the transfer.

This shrinkage during the passage across the Atlantic is due, in part, to the fact that America is so large and thinks so readily in terms of size and space, and is so much more influenced in all its attitudes by the automobile than we are that many of the things it does cannot be copied straight and used in a cut-down form in a smaller and, in several senses of the word, more pedestrian society. They must be thought out afresh from the beginning.

But some of this shrinkage is due also to the dichotomy between the myth and the fact in American life. The image American institutions present is often so different from the reality that when the carbon copies for export actually arrive they are seen to exact a price we are either unable to pay or should be unwilling to meet.

Nor is it only in industry and business that the American stress on bigness and conformity makes itself felt. It is to be found in some places where one might least expect it – in academic life for example, despite the emphasis on the value of the individual in the academic tradition. Emphasis on the group, combined with the immense financial power and prestige of the great Foundations determines the size and scale of much American research, which sometimes seems to bear more relation to the amount of money forthcoming if the project is big enough and impressive enough, than to any intrinsic need for the research itself.

There are, of course, great individual scholars and scientists in America and some fine ones at the head of long-term projects. But there are many who, lacking natural distinction, acquire it by becoming empire builders of research, accumulating to themselves the prestige that accrues to those who head an enormous project. Meanwhile, more modest, but sometimes potentially more valuable, work is allowed to wilt for lack of even the small resources it requires. One may see this same trend, also, in the prestige of the administrator compared with the teacher in many universities. And neither are wholly missing from British academic life. They are creeping up on us.

The emphasis on mass and the group, which has always been present in American society but was previously counteracted to some extent by the value given to the bold and enterprising individual, tends to produce a curious lacuna in the intellectual and spiritual life of the country. One is often struck by what appears to be the separateness of some Americans of the highest quality from the great mass of the nation to which they belong. When one meets them they seem not to have emerged from the totality of their society but to be distinct from it – biological sports, as it were, outside and apart from the main stream of American life. Even at levels much lower than the very highest, one is at times aware of a comparable lacuna. There seems, so to speak, to be no direct relationship between the aspirations, beliefs, and values held by the general body of the nation and those of some of the men and women of lively and intellectually disciplined minds whom one meets, and with whom it is possible to have a genuine conversation because they readily accept the evolutionary view of the nature of opinions and are both interested in ideas and in seeing where they lead.

It is not simply that such men and women have, as is, of course, the case in other societies, many concerns that do not much interest the majority. Nor even that they cannot hope to influence and do not wish to share in much that is happening. Rather, it is as though what is taking place around them takes place quite apart from them in some place with which the communications are down. And this, too, seems to be a consequence of a drive to conformity which it is possible to stand aside from but not to resist.

If all this seems somewhat intangible there are also reasons of a more solid kind why we should regard with caution and restraint the promises of the American invasion. Because we are much smaller and more delicately balanced in our economy than America we simply cannot do some of the things that America does on the scale she does them – and in many instances it is exactly on the scale of the operation that such advantages as there are depend. I do not believe we could take over the values of the American mass-production, mass-consumption, mass-credit society without damage to the social, and even some of the moral values, that years of national and European history have built into our culture. But what is even more certain is that we cannot begin to adopt many of them without making it impossible to survive economically. Unlike America, we depend for our livelihood on the balance of international trade and the precarious relationship between internal consumption and the ability to export. We cannot take a ride on the escalator of constantly rising internal demand by means of which America mounts to ever higher levels of her chain store world without risking falling flat on our faces.

We can have it good so far but no farther unless we want to wreck the economic foundations of that humane, liberal and increasingly fluid society which we have gone some way to building.

For America the consequences of the social course she has set for herself need not be so serious as elsewhere. American society is basically so vigorous, so charged with generosity and optimism, and so confident in its belief in the possibility of change that wrong directions are never final. It is in the nature and character of the land to carry things to excess. But because of the resilience which is the obverse side of this, America's excesses are less likely to be fatal than those of others. Nothing in America is permanent. It is a nation in transition. What it does today can be altered tomorrow. Action and reaction there succeed each other more rapidly than in older countries.

Moreover, because the Americans are more self-consciously American than the English are self-consciously English, or even the French self-consciously French, they still have an intense and youthful interest in the kind of people they are and the kind of society they are making for themselves. They remain eager to take it apart and see what makes it tick.

Because of this they are very capable of discovering their mistakes before too late and doing something about them. Even when one is most aware of the strength of the trend towards conformity in American life one cannot help, also, but be aware of the ferment of writers, sociologists, journalists, students of all kinds, probing and questioning and publishing books full of challenges and denunciations, exhortations, warning and clarion calls, and of the fact that all these challenges, denunciations and exhortations are seized upon and read avidly in their paper-back thousands by an immense number of ordinary people who wish to ask themselves whether it is really so. The pot is stirred constantly. There never comes a time when one has to say: Well this is it, this for good or ill is what American civilization has made of itself.

So long as this ferment, this constant American curiosity about what is happening to themselves, continues, there is no need to worry about America. There is nothing wrong with America that Americans cannot put right.

For other societies, older and less volatile, less rich in resources, less capable of change and with less of the wealth that makes change easy, the danger of swallowing wholesale American ideas, American methods and American values is far greater. If we allow ourselves to accept too much too uncritically we may find ourselves stuck to a degree Americans are not. And in the process we may kill much that gives to English life its colour and zest and character.

I have written a good deal not only about the American invasion but also about America itself. This is because it seems to me important to consider just how far the social and economic ingredients of this invasion have already changed the American dream at home – and to learn if we can.

But of course there is much more to be said than this. It is as difficult to paint a portrait of America as of a man of genius. It is everything one says about it and several score other things too.

In this country I have known some of the most frustrating, exhilarating, oppressive and enlightening experiences of my life. Here, too, I have spent some of the pleasantest hours I can remember.

Often transitory, sometimes commonplace, yet each for some reason – a combination perhaps of time and place and friends – bringing back to me something of the special flavour and zest and colour of America I list some of these memories in my mind: A summer evening in Carmel, long talks in white-frame houses in Georgetown, Washington, the cold fierce grandeur of the Sierra Nevadas and the black fangs of granite through the snow-covered hills, little tucked-away bars in New York, a saloon in Virginia City, hot, hot days in Charleston, South Carolina, cold clear ones in Denver, Colorado, fireflies dancing over the trees in a garden in Philadelphia, the silver lances of the moon striking down to the dark heart of Yosemite, the click of dice and the clatter of the fruit machines at one o'clock in the morning in Harrah's at Lake Tahoe (my wife, who had never seen such things before, to her amazement, hit three jack-pots almost in a row), breakfast at a restaurant on the quayside at Sausaleto, and fishing boats at anchor at Gloucester, Mass., a drive up the switch-back hills of San Francisco in a Thunderbird and along the lake shore at Chicago in another, a house in Berkeley with the quilted carpet of lights along the bay beneath it, and talk beside a fig tree in the garden of another, a picnic in the trees beside the lake at Madison, another on Mount Baker, the long, high whistle of a train across the prairie, and the stillness of a summer afternoon in a garden on the hills above Palo Alto, rain in Portland, Oregon, and a barbecue in Orinda, the blue haze of the mountains of Virginia, a restaurant in Occidental and the sun slanting across the Pacific at Big Sur . . . I could go on and on and on, and add to them a hundred memories of talk and laughter and argument and friendship and disputation all the way across these magnificent, maddening, hospitable, tantalizing United States.

My love affair with America is of long standing. I could not break free from it if I wished. And any man who loves America can find much to trouble his mind about some of the directions its society seems to be taking and some of the things that are done in the name of being a good American.

However, what I have been concerned with in this book is not the America one visits and finds so hard to leave, nor yet the America that the friends I have there live in and grumble about and try to alter and glory in and despair over and are so cynical and so tender about, and to which they owe so deep a fidelity.

What I have been writing about is not the America that looks inward to itself but the America that looks outward to the world: a European's America that sometimes seems altogether too anxious to rebuild the rest of the world, not exactly in its own image, for that would be impossible, but in an image fabricated for export.

America can look after its own achievements and its own mistakes, and no doubt in time it will. It is as the matrix of an exportable new civilization that now moves implacably and steadily nearer to our shores that I have been concerned with it here.

In the course of our history we have borrowed much and assimilated more. But we have not been invaded for nearly a thousand years. However benevolent the American invasion, however rich some of the gifts it brings, however much we may need to accept some of the challenge to our methods it has to offer, let us be sure we are not invaded now.

Appendix

No complete list of the close on 800 American-controlled firms now operating in Britain exists either at the Board of Trade or elsewhere but the following is a representative list of some of the principal companies which are wholly American-owned, or in which there is a substantial American financial interest or which have close management or technical links with American associates in the markets with which they are particularly concerned.

Readers may find it interesting to check the number of products they use or consume at home or work which now have an American parentage.

AT HOME

In the Kitchen

Hoovers Ltd, Bendix Corporation, Sunbeam Electric Ltd, Singer Sewing Machines Ltd, Bakelite Ltd, Ideal Boilers and Radiators Ltd, Crane Ltd, Florence Stoves (these last three supply more than 60 per cent of all the domestic boilers in Britain), Aladdin Industries Ltd, Prestige Group Ltd (Prestige and Skyline cutlery), Colly Ltd, James A. Joblin & Co. Ltd (Pyrex ovenware), Thomas Hedley & Co. Ltd (Tide, Daz, Dreft, Fairy and other soaps and detergents), Colgate-Palmolive, Brillo Manufacturing Co.

In the Larder

Alfred Bird & Sons Ltd (Bird's custard powders, etc.), Standard Brands Ltd, Brown & Polson Ltd (In addition to its brand products this firm produces practically all the starch used in Britain for domestic and manufacturing purposes), H. J. Heinz & Co. Ltd (the famous 57 varieties), Kellogg Co. of Great Britain Ltd, Nabisco Foods Ltd, Quaker Oats Ltd (these last three have a near monopoly of all breakfast cereals consumed in Britain), Kraft Foods Ltd, Swift & Co. Ltd (these two companies produce more than 75 per cent of all the processed cheese eaten), Libby McNeill & Libby Ltd, Carnation Milk Ltd, Mars Ltd (confectionery and chocolate: it also has a subsidiary which makes dog and cat foods).

There are also, of course, a large number of American canned meat and fruit companies whose products find a place in British larders but which are American-based and export to distributors here.

A new development which may have a big impact in British larders is the decision by Safeways Ltd, the second largest supermarket chain in the United States with well over 2,000 stores under its control, to start business in Britain. In January 1962 it established a British subsidiary with an initial capital of £3,000,000 and is now prospecting for sites. In addition to distribution on a mammoth scale Safeways also manufactures canned goods and other food products in the United States as part of its policy of undercutting brand name goods sold by competitors at prices fixed by the manufacturer. It may do the same here.

On the Dressing Table
Elizabeth Arden, Max Factor, Helena Rubenstein, Dorothy Gray, Revlon.

In the Bathroom
Colgate-Palmolive, Toni-Cosmetics Ltd (hair shampoos), Park-Davies Ltd, Gillette Razors Co., Ever Ready Razor Co.

In the Wardrobe
Jantzen Ltd, Spirella Co. of Great Britain Ltd, Gossard Ltd, Twilfit Ltd, Warner Bros. (Corsets) Ltd, Barclay Corsets Ltd, Barclay of Banbury Ltd, International Latex Corporation.

In the Medicine Cupboard

Abbott Laboratories, Bayer Products Ltd, Merck–Sharp & Dohme Ltd, Parke Davis & Co., E. R. Squibb & Sons, Cyanamid Products Ltd, Eli Lilly & Co., Pfizer Ltd, G. D. Searle Ltd, International Chemical Co., Sterling Drug Co., Vick International Ltd, Chesebrough Pond's Ltd, Bristol-Myers Co., Mentholatum Co., Miles Laboratories Ltd, Wm. R. Warner & Co., Evans Chemical Ltd.

Other Household Goods

Yale and Towne Manufacturing Ltd (door locks), Black & Decker Ltd, Stanley Woods (G.B.) Ltd (portable electric tools and do-it-yourself kits), Ronson Ltd, U.K. Time Ltd, Westclox Ltd (clocks and watches), Kodak Ltd, Oreole Records Ltd, Woolworth & Co. Ltd.

AT THE OFFICE

Office Machinery

International Business Machines Ltd. (I.B.M.) Dictaphone Ltd, Remington Rand Ltd, National Cash Register, Burroughs Adding Machines Ltd, Underwood Business Machines, Addressograph Multigraph Ltd, Art Metal Co., Felt and Tarrant Ltd.

Pens, Pencils, Stationery, etc.

Eversharp Ltd, Parker Pen Co., Waterman Pen Co., Eagle Pencil Co., Venus Pencil Co., Easterbrook Hazell Ltd, Columbia Ribbon & Manufacturing Co.

Lifts

Waygood-Otis Ltd.

ON THE ROAD

Cars and other Vehicles

Ford Motor Co. Ltd, Vauxhall Motors Ltd.

Car Accessories
    A. C. Delco, Delco-Remy & Hyatt, Borg-Warner, Champion
Sparking Plug Co.

Tyres
    Goodyear Tyre & Rubber Co., Firestone Tyre & Rubber Co.,
North British Rubber Co.

Petrol and Oil
    Esso Petroleum Ltd, Regent Oil Co., Vacuum Oil Co., Mobil
Oil Ltd.

IN INDUSTRY

Chemicals
    Monsanto Chemicals Ltd, Union Carbide Ltd, American
Cynamid Co., Dow Chemical Co., Du Pont Co. (U.K.) Ltd,
Cabot Carbon Ltd, British Geon Ltd, B. B. Chemical Co.,
Grange Chemicals Ltd.

Precision Instruments
    Sperry-Gyroscope Co. Ltd, Foxborough Yoxall Ltd, Honey-
well-Brown Ltd, Taylor-Short & Mason Ltd, British-American
Optical Co. Ltd, U.K. Optical Bausch & Lomb Ltd.

Metals
    British Aluminium Co., Northern Aluminium Co., Inter-
national Mond Nickel Co.

Abrasives
    Minnesota Mining Corporation, Carborundum Ltd, Norton
Grinding Wheel Ltd.

Electrical and Allied Equipment
    Standard Telephones & Cables Ltd, Sylvania-Thorn Colour
Laboratories, Semi-Conductors Ltd, Eric Resister Ltd.

Engineering and Mining Equipment
Ingersoll-Rand Co., British Timken Ltd, Consolidated Pneumatic Tool Co. Ltd, Joy-Sulivan Ltd, British Jeffrey Diamond Ltd.

Material Handling Equipment
Ruston-Bucyrus Ltd, Yale and Towne Manufacturing Ltd, Blaw Knox Ltd.

Earth Moving
Euclid Co., Caterpillar Tractors Ltd.

Petroleum Refining Machinery
Kellogg Ltd, Foster Wheeler Ltd, Badger Ltd, Procon Ltd, Lummus Ltd.

Printing Machinery
Linotype & Machinery Ltd, Intertype Ltd, Goss Printing Co.

Boots and Shoes Machinery
British United Shoe Machinery Ltd.

ON THE FARM

International Harvester Co. of Great Britain Ltd, Massey-Harris Ferguson Ltd, Allis-Chalmers (Great Britain) Ltd.

THE PERSUADERS

The total extent of American penetration of the British advertising industry is hard to discover. Practically all advertising agencies are private companies and details of shareholdings are difficult to obtain so that no complete record of American investment in British advertising services, which is known to be increasing, is obtainable. According to the *Financial Times* four of the top ten and six of the top fifteen British Agencies were American owned in March 1960.

The following is a list of ten well-known British advertising agencies which are either, like J. Walter Thompson and several others among the biggest, wholly American owned or have, in the words of the *Financial Times*, 'been in effect taken over by American agencies.'

J. Walter Thompson, Erwin Wasey, Ruthrauff & Ryan, McCann-Erickson, S. C. Garland-Compton, Hobson Bates, Pritchard Wood & Partners, Patrick Dolan, Lambe & Robinson, G. Street & Co., Rolls & Parker.

This appendix gives only a short list of some of the main American owned or American affiliated companies now operating in significant sections of the British economy with an indication of the consumer market and specialised business and industrial fields on which they tend to concentrate. I am grateful to the Information Division of the Board of Trade, the Commercial Attache of the U.S. Embassy, the Secretary of the American Chamber of Commerce in London and the Secretary of the Institute of Practitioners in Advertising for their response to my enquiries. None of them are of course in any way responsible for the views expressed in the body of this book with many of which I am sure they would disagree.

Those who are interested in a more detailed examination of American firms in Britain are referred to Dr. John D. Dunning's admirable study 'American Investment in British Manufacturing Industry' (George Allen & Unwin Ltd) in which he analysed in detail the operations of some 205 selected manufacturing companies which are American financed. Although there has been a further steady expansion of American commercial interests in Britain since Dr. Dunning's scholarly analysis was completed in 1957 it remains the most complete survey of the position as a whole yet made. It should be read in conjunction with a shorter study by Dr. Dunning, 'The Present Role of U.S. Investment in British Industry', written for the Spring 1961 edition of 'Moorgate and Wall Street' (published jointly by Philip Hill, Higginson, Erlangers Ltd, London, and Harriman, Riply & Co., Inc., New York).